1989 Pocket Edition

WRECKS & RELICS

Compiled by Ken Ellis

MIDLAND COUNTIES PUBLICATIONS

Contents

. Cover photographs:

Home of the only flying Lightnings, British Aerospace Warton, witnessed a limited outward migration of the former Saudi examples early in 1989. Here Midland Air Museum at Coventry Airport take delivery of their T.55 ZF598 on January 19. (Tim R. Badham)

Forever linked with pioneer aviator A.V. Roe, the Brooklands Museum decided to mark the association with the building of two Avro types ... Roe Biplane BAPC. 187 and a replica of the shed it was housed in! The shed has been sited as close to where the original was as possible. (Ken Ellis)

Seeming very much out of place in the land of much bigger metal, Nord Nora lpha G-ATDB has been out of use at Prestwick Airport for over ten years now. (Alan Curry)

Copyright 1989
Ken Ellis and Midland Counties Publications
ISBN 0 904597 75 X

published by
Midland Counties Publications (Aerophile) Limited
24 The Hollow, Earl Shilton, Leicester, LE9 7NA

Printed in England
by BL & U Printing Limited

Preface

"Why don't you produce it every year?" "It's too bulky to cart it about with me."
"It's far too good to scribble in!" With the arrival of this, the first-ever Pocket
Edition of **Wrecks & Relics**, it is hoped some of these quandaries can be satisfied.
Even if there were enough followers of the subject to justify the issue of a 'big'
edition every year, the compiler is man enough to know he would cope even less with
such demands than he does now!

'New' technology has made this abridged version a reality and I hope that readers
find this a worthwhile addition to the **Wrecks & Relics** 'family'. As ever, I welcome
comments on it. The full volume will go on as usual, and will appear in the early
summer of 1990 covering in massive detail the whole preservation scene with its
review not only of the current situation, but also all the happenings it between it
and the 11th Edition. Depending on the reception of this pocket version, it is
intended to alternate the 'big' volume with the 'mini' version from now on!

Another aim of this version is to encourage new readers (of any age) to the world of
Wrecks & Relics as I am well aware that the structure of the 'big' version may seem
a bit off-putting to the first-time reader. If this tome has caught your interest,
then the Publishers will be only too pleased to talk to you about the 11th Edition
which was still available as the Pocket Edition went to press!

The compilation of the Pocket Edition of **Wrecks & Relics** has relied on the excellent
input of readers all over the country - they will all receive due credit in the 12th
Edition next year. My many thanks to you for your continued support and
encouragement. The burden of checking and refining this edition fell to **Dave
Allport** and to **Tom Poole** and I am indebted to them for their help. Thanks also to
Neil Lewis and Chris Salter at **Midland Counties Publications** for helping to hammer
out the scope of the book and for their continued support of the whole project.

Also published this year is **European Wrecks & Relics,** in the capable hands of Mike
Bursell, and I am sure that I will be joined by many **W&R** readers in welcoming it
into the fold. (Details at the rear.)

Press date for the full-blown 12th Edition of **Wrecks & Relics** is December 31, 1989
and I look forward to hearing from readers old and new, with their views and updates
in due course.

Ken Ellis
May 1989

Myddle Cottage
Welland Terrace
off Mill Lane
Barrowden
Oakham
Leics, LE15 8EH

Notes

S C O P E
Wrecks & Relics Pocket Edition serves to outline briefly the status and whereabouts
of all known **PRESERVED** (ie in museum or other collections, under restoration etc);
INSTRUCTIONAL (ie static airframes in use for training); and **DERELICT** (ie out of use
for a long period of time, fire dump aircraft, scrapped or damaged etc) aircraft in
the United Kingdom and Eire. Where information permits, all aircraft that fall into
these categories at the time of going to press are included, with the following
exceptions :-
[1] airworthy aircraft not part of a specific collection.
[2] aircraft that fall into any of the above categories for only a short period of
    time.
[3] aircraft without provision for a human pilot (unless registered in the BAPC
    system).
[4] in general, aircraft will only be considered if they are at least a cockpit/nose
    section.

E N T R I E S
Entries are all dealt with in a four column-format.
Column One gives the current registration or serial of the aircraft (even if it is
not worn). Aircraft carrying fictitious marks have their registrations or serials
suffixed ", eg G-BKEN" or VZ999". Aircraft are presented civilian first with
military second. Unidentified aircraft are slotted in as appropriate.
Column Two gives an alternative registration or serial, that may help the reader in
identifying the aircraft further, or more positively. Examples : a civilian
identity if a military serial number is worn; a Ministry of Defence 'A' or 'M'
maintenance airframe number (eg A2571 or 8997M); or a British Aircraft Preservation
Council Register of Aircraft identity (eg BAPC 11 - occasionally abbreviated, eg
B'128).
Column Three Aircraft type, often shortened. Some abbreviations appear here,
including : **CIM C**lassroom **I**nstruction **M**odel - a 'proper' airframe (often built on
the production line alongside the 'flyers') intended from scratch to serve as a
grounded instructional airframe; **MPA M**an **P**owered **A**ircraft; **TAD T**raining **A**nd
Demonstration - another variety of CIM.
Column Four Bearing in mind limitations of space, this column gives essentially the
status of the aircraft. Occasionally, it will be used to show other information,
but this is decoded under the appropriate location heading. Regular readers of
Wrecks & Relics should have no problems with these, but to new readers, a brief
outline of most of them follows :
Airworthy (and abbreviated to **a/w**) to denote aircraft within collections or
museums that can be flown.
ATC Air **T**raining **C**orps airframe for instruction or display
BDRT Airframe for **B**attle **D**amage **R**epair **T**raining
Dump Aircraft on a scrap dump
Fire Aircraft with a Fire department for either destructive or non-destructive
fire training use.
Gate Aircraft displayed (normally at a Ministry of Defence establishment) or
'gate guardian' duties or within the base/camp. Please note, that as **Wrecks &
Relics Pocket Edition** goes to press, a whole rash of 'plastic' Hurricanes and
Spitfires were due on the gates of a number of RAF bases. In this case, the
impending device is noted, with space for a 'serial' to be inserted. The real
Spitfires that have left the base are excluded unless their current location is
confirmed (most are to go to St Athan, but some are slated for Shawbury) -
details of these on page 67 and their full movements will of course be charted in
the 12th Edition of **Wrecks & Relics**.
Inst Instructional airframe, used as a teaching/training aid.
PAX tnr Procedure **trainer** to teach escape techniques to passengers (= PAX).

Spares Airframe in use for spares recovery for other aircraft.
Stored Denoting an aircraft that has been out of use for a considerable period
of time (normally twelve months at least)
Restn Airframe under Restoration, or rebuild, to flying condition or to museum
static display condition.
WLT Weapons Loading Trainer.
Wreck Aircraft in poor condition, usually following an accident.
Other words in this column should be self-explanatory.

L O C A T I O N S

Directions to the town or village in question are given after each place name.
Readers should note that these directions are to the town or village mentioned and
not necessarily to the actual site of the aircraft in question. Directions are not
given in the following instances :-
[1] where specific directions to the site are not fully known.
[2] where the location is a large city or town.
[3] where the location is an airfield.
It is felt that for the last two points, readers will be able to find their own way
around! Note also, that at the request of some private owners, some locations have
deliberately been kept vague.

A C C E S S

Unless otherwise stated, all locations in this work are **PRIVATE** and access to them
is **strictly by prior permission**, if **at all**. Museum open times are given as a guide
only and readers are advised to contact the museum in question before setting out
on a journey.

ENGLAND – Avon

BATH
Sea Hawk Restoration Group
WM993	A2522	Sea Hawk FB.5	Spares
WV795	A2661	Sea Hawk FGA.6	Restn
XF113		Swift F.7	Nose

BRISTOL
Bristol City Museum and Art Gallery
Open Monday to Saturday 1000-1700. Queen's Road, Clifton, Bristol BS8 1RL. Tel : 0272 299771.

BAPC 40	Boxkite replica	-

Bristol Industrial Museum
Open Monday-Wednesday & Saturday/Sunday 1000-1300 and 1400-1700. Prince's Wharf, Bristol BS1 4RN. Tel 0272 299771.

XL829	Sycamore HR.14	-

Bristol Plane Preservation Unit
G-AKKB		Gemini 1A	A/w
RG333"	G-AIEK	Messenger 2A	A/w

Brunel Technical College
(Ashley Down, off the A38 north of the city centre) See also Bristol Airport.

G-ATHA	Apache 235	Inst
G-AWBW	Cessna F.172H	Inst
G-AWUK	Cessna F.150H	Inst

Winbolt Collection
Visits by prior application only to Dr G E Winbolt, The Cottage, Castle Road, Pucklechurch, near Bristol, Avon.

XN651	A2616	Sea Vixen FAW.2	Nose

Others (General area)
G-ADPJ		BAC Drone II	Restn
F-BFUT		J/1N Alpha	Restn
MV154	G-BKMI	Spitfire VIII	Restn

BRISTOL AIRPORT
(Or Lulsgate) BTC = Brunel Technical College airframe, see above.

G-ANAP	Dove 6	BTC-Inst
G-ARJW	Apache 160	Spares
G-AVFM	Trident 2E	BTC-Inst
G-AVHN	Cessna F.150G	Wreck
G-AVVW	Cessna F.150H	BTC-Inst
WF410	Varsity T.1	BTC-Inst

FILTON
Airfield
G-BBDG		Concorde 100-002	Spares
WH665	8763M	Canberra T.17	Fire dump

Rolls-Royce Technical School
XF603	Provost T.1	Inst

KEYNSHAM
(On the A4 south east of Bristol)
G-EAVX	B1807	Sopwith Pup	Restn

LOCKING
(On the A371 east of Weston-super-Mare)
WH840	8350M	Canberra T.4	Gate
WL360	7920M	Meteor T.7	Gate
XM708	8573M	Gnat T.1	Gate

WESTON-SUPER-MARE
Woodspring Museum
Open Monday-Saturday 1000-1700 and Bank Holidays. Burlington Street, Weston-super-Mare. Tel 0934 21028

G-BAPS	Campbell Cougar	-

WESTON-SUPER-MARE AIRPORT
International Helicopter Museum
Now fully open - further details from : IHM, White Acre, 75 Elm Tree Road, Locking, Weston-super-Mare, Avon BS24 8EL. Tel 0934 822524.

G-ACWM		Cierva C.30A	Frame
G-ANFH		Whirlwind Srs 1	-
G-ANJV		Whirlwind Srs 3	-
G-AOUJ		Fairey Ultra-Light	-
G-ARVN		Grasshopper 1	-
G-ASHD		Brantly B.2A	-
G-ATBZ	G-17-4	Wessex 60	-
G-ATKV		Whirlwind Srs 3	-
G-AVKE		Gadfly HDW-1	-
G-AVNE	G-17-3	Wessex 60	-
G-AWOX	G-17-2	Wessex 60	-
G-AZBY	G-17-5	Wessex 60	-
G-AZBZ	G-17-7	Wessex 60	-
G-AZYB		Bell 47H-1	-
G-BGHF		WG.30 Series 100	-
G-48/1	G-ALSX	Sycamore III	-
BAPC.128		Watkinson CG-4-IV	MPA
BAPC.153		Westland WG-33	Mock-up
5N-ABW	G-AOZE	Widgeon 2	-
VZ962		Dragonfly HR.1	Spares
WG719	G-BRMA	Dragonfly HR.5	-
XE521		Rotodyne Type Y	Parts
XG452	G-BRMB	Belvedere HC.1	-
XG547	G-HAPR	Sycamore HR.14	-
XG596	A2651	Whirlwind HAS.7	-
XM556	G-HELI	Skeeter AOP.12	Composite
XP165		Scout AH.1	-
XS149		Wessex HAS.3	-
XS463"	XT431	Wasp HAS.1	Composite
XT472		Wessex HU.5	-

Bedfordshire

BEDFORD

Manders Technical College

G-AVCC	Cessna F.172H	Inst

Locally

G-APMM	Tiger Moth	Restn
BGA 400	T.6 Kite 1	Stored

BEDFORD AIRFIELD

(Or Thurleigh) Royal Aerospace Establishment Bedford

G-BBSO		Cherokee 140F	Inst
F-BLEL	G-BFZA	Fournier RF-3	Restn
KB976	G-BCOH	Lancaster X	Stored
KB994		Lancaster X	Fuselage
RF342	G-APRJ	Lincoln 2	Stored
WH872		Canberra T.17	Fire
XG210		Hunter F.6	Inst
XK530		Buccaneer S.2	Stored
XM694		Gnat T.1	Inst
XW626		Comet AEW	Stored

CARDINGTON

Royal Air Force Museum Restoration and Storage Centre

G-AHED	RL962	Dragon Rapide	Stored
BAPC 180		Silver Dart	Stored
BAPC 181	687	BE.2b rep	Underway
F-HMFI		Farman F.40	Stored
N5419	N5419	Bristol Scout	Stored
C4912	G-BLWM	Bristol M.1C	Restn
K4972	1764M	Hart Trainer	Stored
N9899		Southampton I	Fuselage
FE905	LN-BNM	Harvard IIB	Restn
MP425	G-AITB	Oxford I	Restn
VX275	8884M	Sedbergh TX.1	Stored
XE946	7473M	Vampire T.11	Pod
		FE.2b	Nacelle
		Hawker Demon	Frame
	8596M	Horsa	Sections
HA457		Tempest II	Fuselage
8417/18		Fokker D.VII	Restn
		Fi 103 (V-1)	Stored
13064		P-47D-40-RA	Restn

Airship Industries

G-BIHN	Skyship 500	Gondola

CRANFIELD

Arnold Glass

XP514	8635M	Gnat T.1	Stored
XP535	G-BOXP	Gnat T.1	Airworthy
XR987	8641M	Gnat T.1	Stored
XS101	G-GNAT	Gnat T.1	Airworthy
XS452	G-BPFE	Lightning T.5	Stored
XS458		Lightning T.5	Stored
XS898		Lightning F.6	Stored
XS899		Lightning F.6	Stored
XS923		Lightning F.6	Stored

XV328		Lightning T.5	Stored

Cranfield Institute of Technology

G-AWZN		Trident 3B	Inst
G-AZZT		Cherokee 180D	Inst
G-BBOJ		Aztec 250E	Inst
G-BGGY		JetRanger III	Inst
XN979		Buccaneer S.2	Nose-Inst
XT439		Wasp HAS.1	Inst

Vintage Aircraft Team/Militair

Contact : Andrew Picton, 92 Conway Gardens, Grays, Essex RM17 6HG.

G-AIBR		J/1 Autocrat	Frame
G-AKJU		J/1N Alpha	Wreck
G-AMTK		Tiger Moth	Frame
G-ANEH		Tiger Moth	Frame
G-ARSL		Terrier 2	Stored
G-AVCS		Terrier 1	Restn
G-BKRN		Beech D.18S	Stored
G-BMSG	32028	SAAB Lansen	Stored
G-MIOO		Student 2	Restn
G-SHOW		MS.733 Alcyon	Stored
G27-239	'BNCA	Lightning F.2A	Stored
NL985	7015M	Tiger Moth	Frame
TW467	G-ANIE	Auster 5	Airworthy
WE402"	G-VIDI	Venom FB.50	Restn
WR410"	G-BLKA	Venom FB.54	Airworthy
WS760	7964M	Meteor NF.14	Restn
WV686	7621M	Provost T.1	Restn
WZ507	G-VTII	Vampire T.11	Airworthy
XH328		Vampire T.11	Restn
XK416	G-AYUA	Auster AOP.9	Stored
XN637	G-BKOU	Jet Provost T.3	A/w
XP248	7822M	Auster AOP.9	Stored
XP283	7859M	Auster AOP.9	Frame
XS451	8503M	Lightning T.5	Stored
J-1523	G-VENI	Venom FB.50	Stored
J-1632	G-VNOM	Venom FB.50	Stored
91007	G-TJET	Lockheed T-33A	Stored

Others

G-AJIW		J/1N Alpha	Restn
G-AVGU		Cessna F.150G	Spares
G-BDUX		Motor Cadet	Stored

DUNSTABLE

		Pawnee	Frame
BGA 448		DFS Weihe	Stored

EATON BRAY

(3 miles west of Dunstable)

BGA 493	BAPC81	Dagling	Restn
BGA 833		T.8 Tutor	Restn

HATCH

(Off the B658, south west of Sandy)

Skysport Engineering

G-AGOY		Messenger 3	Restn
		Wallace rep	Underway
		Beaufighter TF.X	Restn

H E N L O W
Royal Air Force Museum Storage Site

G-AIZE		Argus II	-
HS503	BAPC 108	Swordfish IV	-
VX461	7646M	Vampire FB.5	-
VX595		Dragonfly HR.1	-
WE982	8781M	Prefect TX.1	-
WV783	7841M	Sycamore HR.12	-
XF785	7648M	Bristol 173	-
8599M	BAPC 109	Cadet TX.1	For sale
		Cadet TX.1	-
		Hawker P.1121	Sections
6130	AJ469	Ventura II	-

Others

BGA 580		EoN Primary	Stored
WT612	7496M	Hunter F.1	Gate
XH278	8595M	Vampire T.11	Gate

Henlow Area

G-ASDK		Terrier 2	Restn
HB-NAV		Pup 150	Fuselage, ATC

O L D   W A R D E N
The Shuttleworth Collection The
Collection is open every day except
Mondays March 1 to December 21.
During the summer months it is open
Monday to Sunday. Times are 1030 to
1730 or dusk if later. Contact :
Shuttleworth Collection, Old Warden
Aerodrome, Biggleswade, Beds, SG18
9EP. Tel 076 727 288.

G-EACN		BAT Bantam	Parts only
G-EBHX		Humming Bird	Static
G-EBIR		DH.51	Airworthy
G-EBJO		ANEC II	Stored
G-EBWD		DH.60X Moth	Airworthy
G-AAIN		Parnall Elf II	A/w
G-AANG	BAPC 3	Bleriot XI	Restn

G-AANH	BAPC 4	Deperdussin	Airworthy
G-AANI	BAPC 5	Blackburn Mono	A/w
G-AAPZ		Desoutter I	Restn
G-AAYX		Southern Martlet	Rest
G-ABAG		DH.60 Moth	Airworthy
G-ABVE		Arrow Active II	A/w
G-ABXL		Archaeopteryx	A/w
G-ADND		Hornet Moth	Airworthy
G-AEBB		Mignet HM.14	Taxiable
G-AEOA		Puss Moth	Airworthy
G-AEXF		Mew Gull	Airworthy
G-AFCL		BA Swallow II	A/w
G-ARSG	BAPC 1	Roe Triplane rep	A/w
G-ASPP	BAPC 2	Boxkite replica	A/w
BAPC 8		Dixon Ornithopter	
			Stored
BAPC 11	No 4	EE Wren	Airworthy
BAPC 37		Blake Bluetit	Restn
D8096	G-AEPH	Bristol F.2b	Airworthy
H5199	G-ADEV	Avro 504K	Airworthy
F904	G-EBIA	SE.5A	Airworthy
K1786	G-AFTA	Tomtit	Restn
K3215	G-AHSA	Tutor	Airworthy
K4235	G-AHMJ	Cierva C.30A	Static
K5414"	G-AENP	Hind (Afghan)	A/w
L8032	G-AMRK	Gladiator I	Airworthy
N5180	G-EBKY	Sopwith Pup	Airworthy
P6382	G-AJRS	Magister I	Airworthy
T6818	G-ANKT	Tiger Moth II	A/w
Z7258"	G-AHGD	Dragon Rapide	A/w
AR501	G-AWII	Spitfire V	Airworthy
WB588	G-AOTD	Chipmunk T.10	A/w
7198/18	G-AANJ	LVG C.VI	Airworthy

S T A N B R I D G E
(3 miles south of Leighton Buzzard)

WP190	8473M	Hunter F.5	Gate

Berkshire

A R B O R F I E L D
(On the A327 south of Reading)
Princess Marina College

XM379		Jet Provost T.3	Fuselage
XM413		Jet Provost T.3	Fuselage
XP244	7864M	Auster AOP.9	Fuselage
XP886		Scout AH.1	Inst
XP899		Scout AH.1	Inst
XR601		Scout AH.1	Inst
XT827		Sioux AH.1	Inst
XV139		Scout AH.1	Inst
XV141		Scout AH.1	Inst
		Gazelle TAD	Inst

B I N F I E L D
(North of the B3034, NW of Bracknell)

G-ASXF		Brantly 305	Stored
G-AYNS		Airmaster H2/B1	Stored
G-BKXH		Robinson R-22	Wreck
G-BLMD		Robinson R-22	Wreck

B R A C K N E L L
RAF Bracknell

XG196	8702M	Hunter F.6A	Gate

John & Maureen Woods

EZ259	G-BMJW	Harvard III	Restn

F I N C H A M P S T E A D		
R I D G E S		
(On the B3016 S of Wokingham) Staravia		
XH362	Vampire T.11	–
XP586	Jet Provost T.4	Fuselage
XP642	Jet Provost T.4	Fuselage
XP669	Jet Provost T.4	Fuselage
XP685	Jet Provost T.4	Fuselage

H A M P S T E A D   M A R S H A L L
(Off the B4009, N of the M4)

G-ANEM	Tiger Moth	Stored

H U N G E R F O R D
Newbury Aeroplane Company

G-AAWO	DH.60G Moth	Restn
G-ACEJ	Fox Moth	Remains
G-ADNE	Hornet Moth	Restn
G-ADRH	Hornet Moth	Restn
G-AFAX VH-ACN	BA Eagle	Restn
G-AFGH	Chilton DW.1	Restn
G-ANTS	Tiger Moth	Restn

M E M B U R Y
Southern Sailplanes

G-AHAG	Dragon Rapide	Stored
G-AHVV	Tiger Moth	Wreck
G-AJHU	Tiger Moth	Wreck
G-AMIU	Tiger Moth	Restn

N E W B U R Y
British Balloon Museum and Library
General enquiries : Secretary BBML, 75
Albany Road, Old Windsor, Berkshire
SL4 2QD.
[All are hot air balloons unless
noted. Column 2 gives state, E=
envelope, B = Basket/Gondola.
Manufacturers = C - Cameron; Ct -
Colt; O - Omega; T - Thunder.]

G-ATGN	E&B Thorn Coal Gas	'Eccles'
G-AVTL	E HAG Free	'Bristol Belle'
G-AWOK	E Sussex Free Gas	'Sardine'
G-AXVU	E O 84	'Henry VIII'
G-AXXP	E&B Bradshaw Free	'Ignis Volens'
G-AYAL	E&B O 56	'Nimble II'

G-AZSP	E C O-84	'Esso'
G-AZUV	E&B C O-65	'Icarus'
G-BAMK	B C D-96	'Isibidbi'
G-BBGZ	E&B Cambridge	'Phlogiston'
G-BCAR	E T Ax7-77	'Marie Antoinette'
G-BCFD	E West	'Hellfire'
G-BCFZ	B C D-500	'Heineken'
G-BETF	E C SS	'Champion'
G-BETH	E T Ax6-56	'Debenhams I'
G-BHKR	E&B C 14A	'Green Ice 5'
G-BIGT	E C 77A	'Big T'
G-ICES	E T Ax6-56 SS	'Fiesta'
G-PNUT	E C SS	'Mr Peanut'
EI-BAY	E C Ax8	'Godolphin'
F-BTVO	E C A-140	'Cumulonimbus'

R E A D I N G
Locally (Various locations)

G-AGNJ VP-YOJ	Tiger Moth		Restn
G-ANDE		Tiger Moth	Wreck
G-ANZT		Jackaroo	Stored
7Q-YMY		Tiger Moth	Restn
WW447		Provost T.1	Stored

T H A T C H A M
(On the A4 east of Newbury)

WV486	7694M	Provost T.1	Spares
XF836	G-AWRY	Provost T.1	Stored
178	G-BKOS	Provost T.51	Restn

T W Y F O R D

SX336	A2055	Seafire XVII	Restn

W H I T E   W A L T H A M

G-AJPI	Argus III	Restn
G-AFGI	Chilton DW.1	Restn

W I N D S O R
Gordon King

B-163	FE930	Harvard IIB	Restn

W O O D L E Y
Bob Ogden/Barry Welford

G-ABZB	Moth Major	Restn
G-AFNI	Moth Minor Coupe	Stored

Buckinghamshire

A Y L E S B U R Y
1365 Squadron ATC, TAVR Centre

XF522	Hunter F.6	Nose

B O O K E R   A I R F I E L D
(Or Wycombe Air Park) Booker Aircraft
Museum Open Saturdays, Sundays and Bank
Holidays, 1030 to 1730. Parties by

appointment. Contact : David King,
Chairman, Booker Aircraft Museum, 3
Spearing Road, High Wycombe,
Buckinghamshire HP12 3JP.

KF435		Harvard IIB	Composite
WV495	7697M	Provost T.1	–
WZ550	7902M	Vampire T.11	–
XA571	7722M	Javelin FAW.1	Nose

XM665	Whirlwind HAS.7	On loan
417657 N99218	B-26K Invader	Nose

Hon Patrick Lindsay Collection
Housed on the airfield, not available
for public inspection.

G-BBII		Fiat G.46	Airworthy
G-BIIZ		Great Lakes 2T-1A	A/w
B4863"	G-BLXT	SE-5E/A	Airworthy
K1930"	G-BKBB	Fury replica	Airworthy
AR213	G-AIST	Spitfire IA	Airworthy
45	G-BHFG	SNCAN SV-4C	Airworthy
120"	G-AZGC	SNCAN SV-4C	Airworthy
1076"	G-AVEB	MS.230	Airworthy

Others

G-BDBL		Chipmunk 22	Cockpit
BAPC 103		Pilcher Hawk	Stored
3460	G-BMFG	Dornier Do 27A-4	Stored
C-499		EKW C-3605	Stored
C-558		EKW C-3605	Stored
		Yak C-11	Frame

D E N H A M

G-OITD	Cessna 310F	Spares

F I N M E R E

G-AWPN	Shield Xyla	Restn

H A L T O N
1 School of Technical Training

G-ASWJ	8449M	Beagle 206 Srs 1	Inst
SL574	8391M	Spitfire XVI	Restn
WT746	7770M	Hunter F.4	Inst
WV276	7847M	Hunter F.4	Inst
WZ559	7736M	Vampire T.11	Pod, dump
XD165	8673M	Whirlwind HAR.10	Inst
XE597	8874M	Hunter FGA.9	Inst
XE656	8678M	Hunter F.6	Inst
XF319	7849M	Hunter F.4	Inst
XF527	8680M	Hunter F.6	Gate
XF974	7949M	Hunter F.4	Inst
XG164	8681M	Hunter F.6	Inst
XG274	8710M	Hunter F.6	Inst
XJ435	8671M	Whirlwind HAR.10	Inst
XJ727	8661M	Whirlwind HAR.10	Inst
XM355	8229M	Jet Provost T.3	Inst
XM362	8230M	Jet Provost T.3	Inst
XM369	8084M	Jet Provost T.3	Dump
XM371		Jet Provost T.3A	Inst
XM375	8231M	Jet Provost T.3	Inst
XM381	8232M	Jet Provost T.3	Inst
XM386	8076M	Jet Provost T.3	Inst
XM402	8055AM	Jet Provost T.3	Nose
XM404	8055BM	Jet Provost T.3	Inst
XM408	8333M	Jet Provost T.3	Inst
XM409	8082M	Jet Provost T.3	Inst
XM411	8434M	Jet Provost T.3	Inst
XM417	8054BM	Jet Provost T.3	Inst
XM467	8085M	Jet Provost T.3	Inst
XM468	8081M	Jet Provost T.3	Inst
XM480	8080M	Jet Provost T.3	Inst

XM706	8572M	Gnat T.1	Inst
XM709	'8617M	Gnat T.1	Inst
XN126	8655M	Whirlwind HAR.10	Inst
XN467	8559M	Jet Provost T.3	Inst
XN512	8435M	Jet Provost T.3	Inst
XN549	8335M	Jet Provost T.3	Inst
XN554	8436M	Jet Provost T.3	Inst
XP354	8721M	Whirlwind HAR.10	Inst
XP405	8656M	Whirlwind HAR.10	Inst
XP442	8454M	Argosy T.2	Inst
XP503	8568M	Gnat T.1	Inst
XP504	8618M	Gnat T.1	Inst
XP511	8619M	Gnat T.1	Inst
XP530	8606M	Gnat T.1	Inst
XP534	8620M	Gnat T.1	Inst
XP540	8608M	Gnat T.1	Inst
XP557	8494M	Jet Provost T.4	Inst
XP567	8510M	Jet Provost T.4	Inst
XP573	8336M	Jet Provost T.4	Inst
XP585	8407M	Jet Provost T.4	Inst
XP640	8501M	Jet Provost T.4	Inst
XP672	8458M	Jet Provost T.4	Inst
XP686	8502M	Jet Provost T.4	Inst
XR140	8579M	Argosy E.1	Fire
XR458	8662M	Whirlwind HAR.10	Inst
XR538	8621M	Gnat T.1	Inst
XR569	8560M	Gnat T.1	Inst
XR574	8631M	Gnat T.1	Inst
XR643	8516M	Jet Provost T.4	Inst
XR650	8459M	Jet Provost T.4	Inst
XR651	8431M	Jet Provost T.4	Inst
XR662	8410M	Jet Provost T.4	Inst
XR670	8498M	Jet Provost T.4	Inst
XR672	8495M	Jet Provost T.4	Inst
XR704	8506M	Jet Provost T.4	Inst
XR953	8609M	Gnat T.1	Inst
XR954	8570M	Gnat T.1	Inst
XR980	8622M	Gnat T.1	Inst
XR984	8571M	Gnat T.1	Inst
XR998	8623M	Gnat T.1	Inst
XS100	8561M	Gnat T.1	Inst
XS109	8626M	Gnat T.1	Inst
XS110	8562M	Gnat T.1	Inst
XS176	8514M	Jet Provost T.4	Inst
XS179	8337M	Jet Provost T.4	Inst
XS180	8338M	Jet Provost T.4	Inst
XS186	8408M	Jet Provost T.4	Inst
XS209	8409M	Jet Provost T.4	Inst
XS210	8339M	Jet Provost T.4	Inst
XS215	8507M	Jet Provost T.4	Inst
XS218	8508M	Jet Provost T.4	Inst
XT257	8719M	Wessex HAS.3	Inst
XX110"	B'169	Jaguar GR.1 rig	Inst
XX118	8815M	Jaguar GR.1	Fuse
XX726	8947M	Jaguar GR.1	Inst
XX739	8902M	Jaguar GR.1	Inst
XX743	8949M	Jaguar GR.1	Inst
XX746	8895M	Jaguar GR.1A	Inst
XX747	8903M	Jaguar GR.1	Inst
XX757	8948M	Jaguar GR.1	Inst

XX818	8945M Jaguar GR.1	Inst
XX956	8950M Jaguar GR.1	Inst
XX966	8904M Jaguar GR.1A	Inst
XX975	8905M Jaguar GR.1	Inst
XX976	8906M Jaguar GR.1	Inst
XZ382	8908M Jaguar GR.1	Inst
XZ389	8946M Jaguar GR.1	Inst

M A R L O W
Staravia Ltd

PH-NLH	Hunter T.7	Stored
E-420 G-9-442	Hunter F.51	Stored

N E W P O R T   P A G N E L L

LA564	Seafire F.46	Restn

P I N E W O O D   S T U D I O S

XP683	Jet Provost T.4	Fuselage
N-202 G-9-223	Hunter F.6	Nose

Cambridgeshire

A L C O N B U R Y

01534"	F-5E mock-up	Gate
60312	F-101B-80-MC	BDRT
63419	F-4C-15-MC	BDRT
66692	U-2CT-LO	Inst
153008	F-4N-MC	BDRT

B A S S I N G B O U R N
Allenbrooke Barracks

WJ821	8668M Canberra PR.7	Display

B O U R N

WP321 G-BRFC	Sea Prince T.1	Stored
	Bell 47G	Wreck
	MBB Bo 105C	Wreck

C A M B R I D G E

G-ASRK	Airedale	Restn
WD356	7625M Chipmunk T.10	Stored

C A M B R I D G E   A I R P O R T
(Or Teversham)

WJ863	Canberra T.4	Nose, fire

C H A T T E R I S
(On the A141 south of March)

G-ARNH	Colt 108	Stored
G-AXNY	Fixter Pixie	Fuselage

D U X F O R D
Imperial War Museum Main season is mid-March to the end of October, 1030 to 1730, with the winter season November to mid-March, 10.30 to 15.45. (Only Superhangar open during winter season) Please note that admission charges vary on flying days. An SAE to the IWM at the address below will bring the latest information on opening times and special events. Contact : Imperial War Museum, Duxford Airfield, Duxford, Cambridge, CB2 4QR. Tel 0223 833963.

The following codes serve to show ownership within the general 'co-operative' at Duxford : IWM - Imperial War Museum; DAS - Duxford Aviation Society; BAM - British Aerial Museum; OFMC - Old Flying Machine Company; TFC - The Fighter Collection; RC - Russavia Collection.

G-ACUU	Cierva C.30A	IWM
G-AFBS	Magister I	IWM
G-AGJG	Dragon Rapide	Restn
G-AGTO	J/1 Autocrat	a/w DAS
G-ALDG	Hermes 4 fuselage	DAS
G-ALFU	Dove 6	DAS
G-ALWF	Viscount 701	DAS
G-ALZO	Ambassador	Restn, DAS
G-ANTK	York	Restn, DAS
G-AOVT	Britannia 312	DAS
G-APDB	Comet 4	DAS
G-APWJ	Herald 201	DAS
G-ASGC	Super VC-10 1151	DAS
G-AVFB	Trident 2E	DAS
G-AXDN	Concorde 01	DAS
G-BFPL	Fokker D.VII rep	a/w, OFMC
G-BOML	Hispano HA.1112	a/w, OFMC
G-HURI	Hurricane IIB	Restn, TFC
G-36-1	SB.4 SHERPA	Stored, IWM
BAPC 90	Colditz Cock	Stored, IWM
BAPC 93 8583M	Fi 103 (V-1)	IWM
CF-EQS	Boeing A75N-1	Stored, IWM
CF-KCG	TBM-3E Avenger	Restn, IWM
F-BCDG	MS.502 Criquet	Stored, IWM
F-BJQC	MS.505 Criquet	a/w, BAM
N47DD	P-47D-30-RA	Restn, IWM
N240CA	F4U-4B Corsair	a/w, OFMC
NC88ZK	Boeing A75N-1	a/w, OFMC
NX700H	F8F-2P Bearcat	a/w, TFC
N6178C	F7F Tigercat	a/w, Lea Av

Reg 1	Reg 2	Type	Status
N6827C		TBM-3E Avenger	a/w, OFMC
N7614C		B-25J-30-NC	Restn, IWM
N8297		FG-1D Corsair	a/w, TFC
N53127		Boeing A75N	OFMC
N62822		P-63C-5-BE	a/w, TFC
N88972		B-25D-30-ND	a/w, TFC
5964"	G-BFVH	DH.2 replica	a/w, RC
E2581		Bristol F.2b	IWM
F3556		RAF RE.8	IWM
K2567"	G-MOTH	Tiger Moth	a/w, RC
N4877	G-AMDA	Anson I	IWM
R3950		Battle I	loan, IWM
V3388	G-AHTW	Oxford I	IWM
V6028"	G-MKIV	Bolingbroke IVT	Wreck, BAM, spares use
V9300	G-LIZY	Lysander III	Restn, BAM
Z2033	G-ASTL	Firefly I	IWM
Z7015	G-BKTH	Sea Hurricane I	Restn, IWM/Shuttleworth
FR870"	NL1009N	P-40N Kittyhawk	a/w, TFC
JV928	G-BLSC	PBY-5A Catalina	a/w, Plane Sailing
KB889	G-LANC	Lancaster X	Restn, IWM
LZ766	G-ALCK	Proctor III	IWM
MH434	G-ASJV	Spitfire IX	a/w, OFMC
ML417	G-BJSG	Spitfire IX	a/w, TFC
ML796		Sunderland MR.5	Restn, IWM
MV293	G-SPIT	Spitfire XIV	Restn, TFC
NF370		Swordfish II	IWM
NH799		Spitfire XIV	Restn, TFC
PN323		Halifax A.VII	Nose, IWM
TA719	G-ASKC	Mosquito TT.35	Restn, IWM
TG263	G-12-1	SARO SR.A.1	IWM
TG528		Hastings C.1A	IWM
TX226	7865M	Anson C.19	Stored, IWM
VT260	8813M	Meteor F.4	Restn, IWM
WD686		Meteor NF.11(mod)	IWM
WF425		Varsity T.1	IWM
WG752		Dragonfly HR.3	IWM
WH725		Canberra B.2	IWM
WJ288	G-SALY	Sea Fury FB.11	Loan, IWM
WJ945	G-BEDV	Varsity T.1	DAS
WK714"	WK914	Meteor F.8	Restn, OFMC
WK991	7825M	Meteor F.8	IWM
WM969	A2530	Sea Hawk FB.5	IWM
WN904	7544M	Hunter F.2	IWM
WZ515		Vampire T.11	Stored, IWM
WZ590		Vampire T.11	IWM
WZ868	G-BCIW	Chipmunk T.10	a/w, RC
XE627		Hunter F.6A	IWM
XF708		Shackleton MR.3/3	IWM
XG577	A2571	Whirlwind HAS.7	Stored, IWM
XG613		Sea Venom FAW.21	IWM
XG743		Sea Vampire T.22	IWM
XG797		Gannet ECM.6	IWM
XH648		Victor B.1A(K2P)	IWM
XH897		Javelin FAW.9	IWM
XJ824		Vulcan B.2A	IWM
XK695		Comet C.2(RCM)	IWM
XK936		Whirlwind HAS.7	IWM
XM135		Lightning F.1A	IWM
XN239	8889M	Cadet TX.3	IWM
XP281		Auster AOP.9	IWM
XR222		TSR-2 XO-4	IWM
XR241	G-AXRR	Auster AOP.9	a/w, BAM
XS576		Sea Vixen FAW.2	IWM
XS863		Wessex HAS.1	IWM
		Typhoon Cockpit,	IWM
A-549	ZD487	FMA Pucara	IWM
671"	G-BNZC	Chipmunk 22	a/w, BAM
9893		Bolingbroke IVT	Stored, IWM
10201	G-BPIV	Bolingbroke IVT	Restn, BAM
18393	G-BCYK	CF.100 Mk IV	IWM
57		Mystere IVA	IWM
92	G-BJGW	Broussard	Restn, BAM
100143		Fa 330A-1	IWM
120235	AM. 68	He 162A-1	IWM
191660	AM.214	Me 163B-1	IWM
6316		Amiot AAC.1	IWM
35075		SAAB J35A Draken	IWM
164"	G-BKGL	Beech 18 3TM	a/w, BAM
592"	G-HAEC	Mustang Mk 22	a/w, OFMC
14286		T-33A-1-LO	IWM
17899		VT-29B-CO	IWM
42165		F-100D-11-NA	IWM
60689		B-52D-40-BW	IWM
226671"	NX47DD	P-47D/N	Airworthy, TFC
231965"	F-BDRS	B-17G-95-DL	IWM
315509	G-BHUB	C-47A-85-DL	IWM
461748	G-BHDK	TB-29A-45-BN	IWM
463221"	N51JJ	P-51D-25-NA	a/w, TFC
485784	G-BEDF	B-17G-105-VE	a/w, B-17 Preservation Ltd
122095		F8F Bearcat	Stored, TFC
133722	N1337A	F4U-7 Corsair	a/w Lindsay Walton
J-1605	G-BLID	Venom FB.50	IWM
		Mitsubishi A6M Cockpit,	IWM
533		Yak C-11	Stored, TFC

Locally

G-NORD	SNCAC NC.854	Stored

E L Y

RAF Hospital

WS774	7959M	Meteor NF.14	Gate

E V E R S D E N

(On the A603 west of Cambridge)

G-ADJJ	Tiger Moth	Stored
G-ATEV	CEA DR.1050	Stored
G-AYBV	YC-12 Tourbillon	Stored
G-AZDY	Tiger Moth	Stored
G-BKKS	Mercury Dart	Stored
F-GAIP 'BKOT	WA.81 Piranha	Stored

H U N T I N G D O N
G-AMNN	Tiger Moth	Wreck
G-BPAJ	Tiger Moth	Restn

K I M B O L T O N
(On the A45 north west of St Neots)
G-ARRG	Cessna 175B	Wreck
VZ477 7741M	Meteor F.8	Nose, School

K I N G S T O N
(On the B1046 west of Cambridge)
G-AKPF	Magister	Restn

L I T T L E   G R A N S D E N
(On the B1046 west of Cambridge)
G-AIRI	Tiger Moth	Stored
G-AWDI	Aztec 250C	Stored

O A K I N G T O N
	Varsity T.1	ATC, nose

S I B S O N
(Or Peterborough Sport Airfield)
G-AWSD	Cessna F.150J	Wreck
G-BABD	Cessna FRA.150L	Fuselage
G-BCRA	Cessna F.150M	Fuselage
G-BDFJ	Cessna F.150M	Wreck
G-BFWF	Cessna 421B	Stored
G-BLSS	Cessna F.150J	Fuselage
G-HUNY	Cessna F.150G	Wreck
WW444	Provost T.1	Restn

W H I T T L E S E Y
(On the A605 east of Peterborough)
G-AOGV	J/5R Alpine	Stored

W I L L I N G H A M
(South of the A1123, east of Huntingdon)
G-ARAU	Cessna 150	Stored

W I S B E C H
<u>Fenland Aircraft Preservation Society</u>
Museum display now open, contact : 14 Millway, Fridaybridge, Wisbech, Cambs PE14 0HZ.
XD434	Vampire T.11	-

W I T T E R I N G
	Spitfire replica	Gate
XF383 8706M	Hunter F.6	BDRT
XV279 8566M	Harrier GR.1	WLT
XV281	Harrier GR.1	Spares
XV779 8931M	Harrier GR.3	Gate
XW923 8724M	Harrier GR.3	Nose

W Y T O N
WH773 8696M	Canberra PR.7	Gate
WH848	Canberra T.4	Inst
WJ817 8695M	Canberra PR.7	Fire
WK127	Canberra TT.18	BDRT
WT305 8511M	Canberra B.6(mod)	Gate
XH170 8739M	Canberra PR.9	Gate
	Canberra PR.3/T.4	Nose, dump
	Canberra T.4	Nose

Cheshire

C H E L F O R D
(On the A357 east of Knutsford) <u>Macclesfield Historical Aviation Society</u> Vistors welcome, contact for details : MHAS, 17 Pitt Street, Macclesfield, SK11 7PT.
WH850	Canberra T.4	-
XE584	Hunter FGA.9	Nose
XR654	Jet Provost T.4	Fuselage

<u>Locally</u>
EI-BRY	Cessna 210M	Wreck

C H E S T E R
XH312	Vampire T.11	Restn

C O N G L E T O N
G-ACOJ F-AMXP	Leopard Moth	Restn
G-ACOL HB-OXO	Leopard Moth	Restn

H A N D F O R T H
<u>395 Squadron ATC</u>
WZ869 8019M	Chipmunk T.10	PAX tnr

M A C C L E S F I E L D
<u>Lovaux Ltd</u>
WJ722	Canberra B.2	Dismantled
XJ690	Hunter FGA.9	Fuselage
XV155	Buccaneer S.2B	Stored
ET-272 G9-430	Hunter T.7	Dismantled

<u>Macclesfield College of Further Education</u>, Park Street.
XD624	Vampire T.11	Inst

M A L P A S
(East of the A41 north west of Whitchurch) <u>617 Squadron ATC</u>, Malpas School.
XK944 A2607	Whirlwind HAS.7	-

SAIGHTON
(Off the A41 south of Chester)
Saighton Camp
XS521   Wessex HU.5   Inst

WARMINGHAM
(South of Middlewich in between the A530 and the A533) The Aeroplane Collection At the Warmingham Craft Centre, The Old Mill. The Craft Centre is open 1000 to 1700 weekdays and 1000 to 1800 at weekends. TAC can be contacted at : 7, Mayfield Avenue, Stretford, Manchester M32 9ML. Tel 061 865 0665
G-BLHL   CP.301A Emeraude   Restn
BAPC 15   Addyman STG   -

BAPC 192	Weedhopper JC-24	-
BAPC 193	Hovey Whing Ding	-
	Chrislea Skyjeep	Frame
XK819	Grasshopper TX.1	-
XL811	Skeeter AOP.12	-
XN298	Whirlwind HAR.9	-

WARRINGTON
1330 Squadron ATC
XM474   8121M Jet Provost T.3   Nose

WILMSLOW
G-APVU   L.40 Meta-Sokol Stored

WINSFORD
(On the A54 south of Northwich)
G-ASFB   Musketeer 23   Wreck

Cleveland

TEES-SIDE AIRPORT
(Or Middleton St George) Civil
Aviation Authority Fire School

G-ARPD	Trident 1C	Poor state
G-ARPO	Trident 1C	Whole
G-ARPR	Trident 1C	Poor state
G-ARPW	Trident 1C	Whole
G-AVFJ	Trident 2E	Whole
G-AWZR	Trident 3B-101	Whole
G-AWZS	Trident 3B-101	Whole
G-AZLP	Viscount 813	Whole
G-AZLS	Viscount 813	Whole
D-IOMI	Aztec 250	Wreck
XP330	Whirlwind HAR.10	Gutted

Cornwall

CALLINGTON
(On the A390 south west of Tavistock)
XR755   Lightning F.6   -

CHACEWATER
(East of the A30, north east of Redruth)
G-ARWY   Mooney M.20A   Wreck
G-BTSC   Evans VP-2   Stored

CULDROSE
HMS 'Sea Hawk' ETS = Engineering Training School SAH = School of Aircraft Handling

WF225	A2645	Sea Hawk F.1	Gate
WT711		Hunter GA.11	SAH
WT804		Hunter GA.11	SAH
WV267		Hunter GA.11	SAH
WW654		Hunter GA.11	SAH
XE668		Hunter GA.11	SAH
XM328		Wessex HAS.3	SAH
XM870		Wessex HAS.3	SAH
XP137		Wessex HAS.3	SAH
XP980	A2700	Hawker P.1127	SAH
XS695	A2619	Kestrel FGA.1	SAH
XS866	A2705	Wessex HAS.1	SAH
XS876	A2695	Wessex HAS.1	SAH
XS877	A2687	Wessex HAS.1	ETS
XS885	A2668	Wessex HAS.1	SAH
XT762		Wessex HU.5	SAH
XV588		Phantom FG.1	Nose
XV669	A2659	Sea King HAS.1	ETS
XX466		Hunter T.7	SAH

HELSTON
Flambards Triple Theme Park
Open every day Easter to October 1000 to 1700, further details from Flambards Triple Theme Park, Clodgey Lane, Helston, Cornwall, TR13 0GA. Tel 03265 3404.

G-APTW	Widgeon	-
G-BDDX	MW.2B Excalibur	-
BAPC 116	Demoiselle replica	-
BAPC 129	Blackburn 1911 rep	Stored
BAPC 130	Blackburn 1912 rep	Stored
F5459"BAPC142	SE.5A replica	-
WF122 A2673	Sea Prince T.1	-

WF299	WN105	"Sea Hawk FB.3	Composite
WG511		Shackleton T.4	Nose
WG725	N9987Q	Dragonfly HR.5	-
WV106		Skyraider AEW.1	-
XA870	A2543	Whirlwind HAS.1	-
XD332	A2574	Scimitar F.1	-
XE368	A2534	Sea Hawk FGA.6	-
XG691		Sea Venom FAW.22	-
XG831	A2539	Gannet ECM.6	-
XJ917		Sycamore HR.14	-
XN258		Whirlwind HAR.9	-
XN647	A2610	Sea Vixen FAW.2	-
XN967	A2627	Buccaneer S.1	-
XP350		Whirlwind HAR.10	-
XS887	A2690	Wessex HAS.1	-
XT427		Wasp HAS.1	-

L A N D ' S   E N D   A I R P O R T
(Or St Just)

G-ARZD	Cessna 175C	Wreck
G-AYMF	Airtourer	Wreck
G-AZTN	Airtourer	Wreck

L E L A N T
(On the A3074 south of St Ives)

| G-ABTC | Comper Swift | Stored |

L I S K E A R D

| XS936 | Lightning F.6 Castle Air |

L O W E R   T R E M A R
(North of Liskeard)

| XR751 | Lightning F.6 | - |
| XS919 | Lightning F.6 | - |

P E R R A N P O R T H

| | Olympia | Stored |

P R E D A N N A C K
Royal Navy Fire School

WF125	A2674	Sea Prince T.1	-
XE712		Hunter GA.11	-
XL836	A2642	Whirlwind HAS.7	-
XL846	A2625	Whirlwind HAS.7	-
XM329	A2609	Wessex HAS.1	-
XM331		Wessex HAS.3	Poor state
XM838		Wessex HAS.1	-
XM841		Wessex HAS.1	Poor state
XN934	A2600	Buccaneer S.1	-
XN953	8182M	Buccaneer S.1	-
XP107	A2527	Wessex HAS.1	-
XP149	A2669	Wessex HAS.1	-
XS119		Wessex HAS.3	-
XS125	A2648	Wessex HAS.1	-
XT441	A2703	Wasp HAS.1	-
XT450		Wessex HU.5	-
XT757	A2722	Wessex HU.5	-

S T   M A W G A N

A1742"	BAPC38	Bristol Scout replica
		travelling exhibit
D34192	BAPC59	Sopwith Camel replica
		travelling exhibits
WJ870	8683M	Canberra T.4	BDRT
WL795	8753M	Shackleton AEW.2	Gate
XH132	8915M	Short SC-9	BDRT

S T   M E R R Y N

| G-MLAS | Cessna 182E | Para-tnr |
| G-STMP | SNCAN SV-4A | Stored |

Cumbria

C A R K

| G-AWMZ | Cessna F.172H | Para-tnr |

C A R L I S L E
RAF Kingstown (On the A7 north of the City)

WS792	7965M	Meteor NF.14	Gate
WT660	7421M	Hunter F.1	Gate
XT255	8751M	Wessex HAS.3	BDRT

C A R L I S L E   A I R P O R T
(Or Crosby-on-Eden) Solway Aviation Society SAS aircraft and the privately owned Vulcan open to inspection Sundays 1300 to 1700. Further details : 27 St Martin's Drive, Brampton, Cumbria CA8 1TQ.

| G-BAYY | Cessna 310C | Fire |
| WE188 | Canberra T.4 | Solway |

WS832		Meteor NF.14	Solway
XJ823		Vulcan B.2A	-
ZF583	53-681	Lightning F.53	Solway

S P A D E A D A M
(North of the B6318, north east of Carlisle) RAF Weapons Range (WR)/Electronic Warfare Site (EWS)

FT-01	T-33A-1-LO	WR
FT-02	T-33A-1-LO	EWS
FT-06	T-33A-1-LO	EWS
FT-07	T-33A-1-LO	EWS
FT-10	T-33A-1-LO	EWS
FT-11	T-33A-1-LO	EWS
FT-29	T-33A-1-LO	WR
61	Mystere IVA	EWS
64	Mystere IVA	EWS
81	Mystere IVA	EWS
139	Mystere IVA	EWS

180		Mystere IVA	EWS
		Mystere IVA	EWS
		Mystere IVA	EWS
		Mystere IVA	EWS

W I N D E R M E R E
Windermere Steamboat Museum, Rayrigg Road, open Easter to October, Monday to Saturday 1000 to 1800 and 1400 to 1800 on Sundays. Windermere Steamboat Museum, Rayrigg Road, Windermere, Cumbria LA23 1BN. Tel 096 62 5565.

| BGA.266 | T.1 Falcon | - |

Derbyshire

B U X T O N

| BGA 1999 | DCB Fauvel AV.36CR | Stored |

H A D F I E L D
(On the A621 east of Greater Manchester) Military Aircraft Preservation Group Contact : Phil Maloney, 51 Bleak Hey Road, Peel Hall, Wythenshawe, Manchester M22 5FS.

| XD534 | Vampire T.11 | Pod |
| 333 | Vampire T.55 | Pod |

Others

| G-ANFC | | Tiger Moth | Restn |
| VP519 | G-AVVR | Anson C.19/2 | Nose |

S H A R D L O W
(On the A6 south east of Derby)

| G-ATGZ | Griffiths GH.4 | Stored |

Devon

C H I V E N O R

WJ629	8747M	Canberra TT.18	BDRT
WJ635		Canberra B.2	Nose
WT806		Hunter GA.11	Airworthy
XD186	8730M	Whirlwind HAR.10	Gate
XF509	8708M	Hunter F.6A	Gate
XL567	8723M	Hunter T.7	Fire
XX257		Hawk T.1	BDRT

D U N K E S W E L L

| WV679 | 7615M | Provost T.1 | Restn |

E X E T E R
Local Store

G-AALP	Surrey AL.1	Stored
G-AFGC	BA Swallow II	Stored
G-AFHC	BA Swallow II	Stored

Elsewhere

| FT323" | 1513 | Harvard II | Restn |

E X E T E R   A I R P O R T

G-AHAT		J/1N Alpha	Stored
G-AMZY		Dove 8XC	Fire
G-ASRX		Queen Air A80	Spares
G-AYTC		Aztec 250C	Spares
G-BASU		Navajo 350	Fuselage
EI-BSI	N3455	C-47B Dakota	Stored
N500LN		Howard 500	Stored
VH-BLF		Debonair	Wreck

H I G H E R   B L A G D O N
Torbay Aircraft Museum Is currently seeking new premises in the Torbay area and will not be open for the time being. Several aircraft are held in store, but are not available for inspection at present.

BAPC 69		Spitfire replica	-
BAPC 74		'Bf 109' replica	-
BAPC167		SE.5A replica	-
L1592" BAPC63		Hurricane replica	-
		Varsity T.1	Cockpit
425/17"BAPC133		Fokker Dr I replica	-
100545		Fa 330A-1	On loan

M A N A D O N
Royal Naval Engineering College, HMS 'Thunderer'

XF321		Hunter T.7	-
XL879		Whirlwind HAS.7	Cockpit
XP984	A2658	Hawker P.1127	-
XS122	A2707	Wessex HAS.3	-
XS153		Wessex HAS.3	-
XV625		Wasp HAS.1	-
XW839		Lynx 00-05	-
XZ249		Lynx HAS.1	Wreck

M O R E T O N H A M P S T E A D
(On the A382 north west of Newton Abbot)
G-AIPW   J/1 Autocrat   Restn

W E M B U R Y
Weapons Range, south of Plymouth.
XP748   8446M Lightning F.3   -

Dorset

B L A N D F O R D   F O R U M
G-BIUP   SNCAN NC.854S   Stored

B O U R N E M O U T H
FX442   Harvard II   Restoration
               Auster   Stored

B O U R N E M O U T H   A I R P O R T
(Or Hurn)
Jet Heritage Ltd
G-BOOM G9-432 Hunter T.7   Airworthy
G-GONE J-1542 Venom FB.50   Airworthy
G-JETP   Jet Provost T.52A   a/w
G-PROV   Jet Provost T.52A   a/w
G-SEAH WM994 Sea Hawk FB.5   Restn
WM167 G-LOSM Meteor TT.20   Airworthy
XF114   Swift F.7   Restn
XL572   8834M Hunter T.7   Stored
XL617   8837M Hunter T.7   Stored
XR658   8192M Jet Provost T.4   Restn
Lovaux Ltd
G-BNCX XL621 Hunter T.7   Stored, a/w
XJ690" XG195 Hunter FGA.9   Composite
E-402 G-9-433 Hunter F.51   Inst
QA-10 G-9-286 Hunter FGA.78   Stored
QA-12 G-9-284 Hunter FGA.74   Stored
Others
G-ASLH   Cessna 182F   Restn
G-ASLL   Cessna 336   Stored
G-ATAH   Cessna 336   Stored
G-ATLC   Aztec 250C   Stored
G-AVDR   Queen Air B80   Stored
G-AVDS   Queen Air B80   Stored
G-BEZB   Herald 209   Spares
G-BNNG G-COLD Cessna T.337D   Rebuild
G-VIXN XS587 Sea Vixen FAW.2TT Stored
G-17-6 G-AWXX Wessex 60   Stored
EL-AJC   Boeing 707-430   Fire
N1721Z   Cessna 336   Wreck
WH911   Canberra B.2   Stored
1190   Bf 109E   Restoration
150225"G-AYNC Wessex 60   Stored

B O V I N G T O N
(Off the A352 near Wool, west of Wareham) Junior Leaders Regiment
XM564   Skeeter AOP.12   Gate

C H R I S T C H U R C H
XJ580   Sea Vixen FAW.2 Display

D O R C H E S T E R
Wessex Aviation & Transport Collection
G-ABEV   DH.60G Moth   Airworthy
G-ACZE   Dragon Rapide   Airworthy
G-ADHA   Fox Moth   Airworthy
G-ADPS   Swallow II   Airworthy
G-AFOB   Moth Minor   Airworthy
G-AGAT   J3F-50 Cub   Airworthy
G-AIYS   Leopard Moth   Airworthy
G-AZMH   MS.500 Criquet   Airworthy
G-BMNV   SNCAN SV-4L   Airworthy
N4712V   PT-13D Kaydet   Airworthy
T5672 G-ALRI Tiger Moth   Airworthy
V9281" G-BCWL Lysander IIIA   Airworthy
Tim Lane
TW439 G-ANRP Auster 5   Restn

P O R T L A N D
XT786   A2726 Wasp HAS.1   Fire, poor
XV623   A2724 Wasp HAS.1   Fire
XV624   Wasp HAS.1   Fire

S H E R B O R N E
(On the A30 east of Yeovil) Westland
Customer Training School
G-BIWY   WG.30-100   Inst
              'Gyrocopter'   Inst
XR526   8147M Wessex HC.2   Inst
PA-12 ZE449 SA.330L Puma   Inst

WEST MOORS
(On the B3072 north of Bournemouth)
RAOC Fuel Department
XS535   Wasp HAS.1   Fire

Essex

ANDREWSFIELD
(Or Great Saling)

G-AXTK	Cherokee 140B	Wreck

AUDLEY END

NF875	G-AGTM	Dragon Rapide	Restn

BASILDON
2243 Squadron, ATC

G-AWVH	Airtourer T.2	Inst

CHELMSFORD
276 Squadron, ATC, Meteor Lane

WH132	7906M	Meteor T.7	-

Elsewhere

G-ANPK	Tiger Moth	Restn

DOWNHAM
(North east of Billericay)

G-ACBH	2895M	Blackburn B-2	Fuselage

EARLS COLNE
Rebel Air Museum Not yet open, details from : 14 Amyruth Road, Brockley, London, SE4 1HQ.

BAPC 115	HM.14 Pou du Ciel	-
N9606H	PT-26 Cornell II	-
	Meteor	Nose
319	Mystere IVA	-

Elsewhere

705	G-OYAK	Yak 18	Restn
TD248	7246M	Spitfire XVI	Restn

EAST TILBURY
Thameside Aviation Museum Opening details : 80 Elm Road, Grays, Essex, RM17 6LD.

G-ADXS	HM.14 Pou du Ciel	-

FOULNESS ISLAND
Proof and Experimental Establishment

WE121		Canberra B.2/8	-
WH673		Canberra B.2	Fuselage
WJ643		Canberra B.2/8	Noseless
WJ679		Canberra B.2	-
WJ872	8492M	Canberra T.4	Noseless
WJ880	8491M	Canberra T.4	Noseless
WJ990		Canberra B.2	-
WK164		Canberra B.2E	Fuselage
WT507	8548M	Canberra PR.7	Noseless
WT534	8549M	Canberra PR.7	Noseless
WT859	A2499	Supermaine 544	Fuselage
XD215	A2573	Scimitar F.1	Fuselage
XD219		Scimitar F.1	Fuselage
XD235		Scimitar F.1	Fuselage
XD241		Scimitar F.1	Fuselage
XD244		Scimitar F.1	Fuselage
XD267		Scimitar F.1	Fuselage
XD322		Scimitar F.1	Fuselage
XD333		Scimitar F.1	Fuselage
XD857		Valiant BK.1	Nose
XK525		Buccaneer S.1	Fuselage
XM271	8204M	Canberra B(I).8	F'lage
XN259	A2604	Whirlwind HAS.7	-
XN726	8545M	Lightning F.2A	-
XN771		Lightning F.2A	-
XN795		Lightning F.2A	-
XN955		Buccaneer S.1	Fuselage
XN960		Buccaneer S.1	Fuselage
XR756		Lightning F.6	-
XS421		Lightning T.5	Fuselage
XS565		Wasp HAS.1	-
XS927		Lightning F.6	-
XV280		Harrier GR.1	Fuselage
XV357		Buccaneer S.2A	-
XV373		Sea King HAS.1	-
XV417		Phantom FGR.2	Wreck
XV798		Harrier GR.1	Engine test rig
XW541	8858M	Buccaneer S.2B	-
XW837		Lynx 1-06	-
XX153		Lynx AH.1	-
XX510		Lynx HAS.2	-
	WAE.32	Lynx rotor rig	-

FYFIELD
(On the B184 west of Chelmsford)

N3850K	Cherokee 140	Fuselage

HALSTEAD
(North east of Braintree)

G-APBI	Tiger Moth	Restn

NAVESTOCK
(Between the A113 and A128 south of Chipping Ongar)

G-AFOJ	Moth Minor	Stored

NORTH WEALD
Aces High Flying Museum Visits by prior permission only. Contact : 037 882 2949. Other enquiries to : Aces High, Building D2, Fairoaks Airport, Chobham, Surrey. Tel 09905 6384.

G-AWHB		CASA 2-111	Stored
		JetRanger	Static
D-TABX	"G-BFHG	CASA 352L	Airworthy
NC75WB	G-BKRG	Beech C-45G	Static
N212DM	G-BPFY	PBY-5A Catalina	Airworthy
N506DM		Seneca 200	Airworthy
N999PJ		MS.760 Paris	Airworthy
N1042B		B-25 Mitchell	Airworthy
N2700	G-BLSW	C-119G Boxcar	Static
N3267U		C-119G Boxcar	Stored

EN398"BAPC184	Spitfire IX rep	Static
HD368" N9089Z	TB-25J-NC	Static
WF877	Meteor T.7(mod)	Static
XS104 8604M	Gnat T.1	Restn
503	MiG-21PF	Stored
J-1758 N203DM	Venom FB.54	Airworthy
100884 G-DAKS	Dakota 3	Airworthy
483009"	AT-6D Harvard	Static

The Squadron/Harvard Formation Team Membership enquiries to : The Squadron, North Weald Airfield, Epping, Essex CM16 1AA

G-AZSC	Harvard IIB	Airworthy
G-ONAF N45192	NAF N3N-3	Airworthy
N15799	Texan/'Zeke'	Airworthy
EX280 G-TEAC	Harvard IIA	Airworthy
FE992 G-BDAM	Harvard IIB	Airworthy
FT239 G-BIWX	Harvard IV	Airworthy
HB275" N5063N	Beech D.18S	Airworthy
B-168	Harvard IIB	Spares

Robs Lamplough

G-BMFB	AD-4W Skyraider	Stored
G-BMFC	AD-4W Skyraider	Stored
G-BMJY	Yak C-18M	Restn
G-KYAK	Yak C-11	Airworthy
BAPC 136	Deperdussin rep	Stored
BAPC 141	Macchi M.39	Stored
S1595"BAPC156	Supermarine S.6	Stored
MV370 G-FXIV	Spitfire XIV	Static
20385" G-BGPB	Harvard IV	HFT/a/w
152/17"G-ATJM	Fokker Dr I rep	a/w
28	P-51D-20-NA	Restoration
72216 G-BIXL	P-51D-20-NA	Airworthy
126912	AD-1N Skyraider	Stored

North Weald Aircraft Restoration Flight Contact : North Weald Aircraft Restoration Flight, North Weald Airfield, Epping, Essex. Tel 01 521 7683.

BAPC 117	RAF BE.2 replica	Stored
BAPC 179	Sopwith Pup rep	Stored
V7767" BAPC72	Hurricane replica	Stored
WJ880 8491M	Canberra T.4	Nose
WM311" WM224	Meteor TT.20	-
XK625	Vampire T.11	Stored
C19/18"BAPC118	Albatros replica	Stored
	Hunter	Nose section

PAGLESHAM
(North east of Rochford)

G-BFEX	Pawnee 235D	Wreck
N5595K	Beaver	Stored

SOUTHEND
Southend Historic Aircraft Society

G-AEZF	Scion II	Restoration

SOUTHEND AIRPORT
(Or Rochford)

G-AIJZ	J/1 Autocrat	Restn
G-AOHL	Viscount 802	Cabin tnr
G-AOHT	Viscount 802	Stored
G-APBW	Auster 5	Restn
G-APEX	Viscount 806	Poor state
G-APWA	Herald 100	Poor state
G-ARAB	Cessna 150	Wreck
G-ASYN	Terrier 2	Spares
G-ATMN	Cessna F.150F	Spares
G-AVWZ	Fournier RF-4D	Fuselage
G-AVZO	Pup 100	Fuselage
G-AWCK	Cessna F.150H	Wreck
G-AWLJ	Cessna F.150H	Wreck
G-AWOC	MS.892A Rallye	Wreck
G-AYOX	Viscount 814	Fuselage
G-AYRK	Cessna 150J	Stored
G-AYYE	Cessna F.150L	Spares
G-AZDZ	Cessna 172K	Wreck
G-AZRW	Cessna T.337C	Stored
G-BCAB	MS.894A Rallye	Wreck
G-BCTH	Cherokee 140	Wreck
G-BDOZ	Fournier RF-5	Stored
G-BEPE G52-14	Belfast	Spares use
G-BEYE	Herald 401	Stored
G-BKME	Skyvan 3-100	Stored
G-MAST	Cherokee 180	Wreck
N4806E	B-26C Invader	Restn
4X-AVB	Viscount 833	Spares
4X-AVF	Viscount 831	Spares
XG325	Lightning F.1	Nose, ATC
XL426 G-VJET	Vulcan B.2A	Stored
XR363 G-OHCA	Belfast C.1	Stored

STANSTED AIRPORT

G-ANPP	Proctor III	Restn
G-ANUW	Dove 6	Stored
G-APFG	Boeing 707-436	Fuselage
G-AWZU	Trident 3B-101	Fire
5N-AVR	DC-8-55	Spares use
5Y-AXC	Boeing 707-351C	Stored

STAPLEFORD TAWNEY

G-AXGD	MS.880B Rallye	Stored
EI-BIE G-STAP	Cessna FA.152	Restn

STONDON
(Off the A128 south east of Chipping Ongar)

G-APWU	Tawney Owl	Stored

Gloucestershire

COLEFORD
(On the A4136 east of Monmouth)

BAPC.46	HM.14 Pou du Ciel	-

FAIRFORD

37699	F-4C-21-MC	BDRT

GLOUCESTER / CHELTENHAM AIRPORT
(Or Staverton)

G-ACSP		DH.88 Comet	Restn
G-AJOE		Messenger 2A	Restn
G-AMBB		Tiger Moth	Restn
G-DACA	WF118	Sea Prince T.1	Stored
G-GACA	WP308	Sea Prince T.1	Stored
G-RACA	WM735	Sea Prince T.1	Stored
N46EA	XK885	Pembroke C.1	Stored
WL349		Meteor T.7	Display

INNSWORTH
(West of the B4063, near Parton, north east of Gloucester - RAF Innsworth)
Cotswold Aircraft Restoration Group
Visits by prior permission only, contact :- Steve Thompson, CARG, Kia-Ora, Risbury, Leominster, Herefordshire, HR6 0NQ.

G-ADRG"BAPC77		HM.14 Pou du Ciel	-
G-ASIP		Auster 6A	Spares
R9371		Halifax II	Cockpit
VW453	8703M	Meteor T.7	Restn
XG331		Lightning F.1	Nose
XK421	8365M	Auster AOP.9	Spares
XN412		Auster AOP.9	Stored
XR267	G-BJXR	Auster AOP.9	Restn
XW264		Harrier T.2	Nose
		Tiger Moth	Frame

Gate Guardian

XH903	7938M	Javelin FAW.9	-

KEMBLE

WH364	8169M	Meteor F.8	Gate
01532		F-5E Tiger II	Stored
01535		F-5E Tiger II	Stored
01543		F-5E Tiger II	Stored
01549		F-5E Tiger II	Stored
01551		F-5E Tiger II	Stored
01553		F-5E Tiger II	Stored
01559		F-5E Tiger II	Stored
01560		F-5E Tiger II	Stored
01566		F-5E Tiger II	Stored
01569		F-5E Tiger II	Stored

MORETON-IN-THE-MARSH
(On the A44 north east of Cheltenham)

BGA.964	Kranich II	-
	Hutter H.17a	Restn
BAPC.25	Nyborg TGN.III	Restn

QUEDGELEY
(On the A430 south of Gloucester)

WF784	7895M Meteor T.7	Gate

STONEHOUSE
(On the B4008 west of Stroud)

XE979	Vampire T.11	Poor state

STROUD
1329 Squadron, ATC, Bowbridge Lane.

WP845	Chipmunk T.10	PAX tnr

Hampshire

ALDERSHOT
Airborne Forces Museum at Browning Barracks, east of the A325 immediately south of Farnborough airfield. Open every day except Christmas Day, Monday to Friday 0900 to 1230 and 1400 to 1630; Saturday 0930 to 1230 and 1400 to 1630; Sunday 1000 to 1230 and 1400 to 1630. Contact : The Airborne Forces Museum, Browning Barracks, Aldershot, Hampshire, GU11 2DS. Tel : 0252 24431 ext 4619.

KP208	Dakota IV	-
	Hotspur II	Nose
	Horsa II	Nose

ANDOVER
The Durney Collection Contact : 276 Weyhill Road, Andover, Hampshire.

G-ALAX	Dragon Rapide	Restn

CHILBOLTON

G-AVKY	Hiller UH-12E	Wreck
G-AZSV	Hiller UH-12E	Cabin

G-BBLD		Hiller UH-12E	Wreck
G-BDFO		Hiller UH-12E	Cabin
G-BEDK		Hiller UH-12E	Cabin
G-BGFS		W-Bell 47G-3B1	Stored
G-BGOZ		W-Bell 47G-3B1	Wreck
AP-AWQ		Hiller UH-12E-4	Cabin

FARNBOROUGH
Royal Aerospace Establishment

G-ANNG		Tiger Moth	Stored
G-AZGJ		MS.880B Rallye	Restn
BGA.562		Olympia 1	Stored
		Broburn Wanderlust (glider)	Stored
WE146		Canberra PR.3	Nose
WJ865		Canberra T.4	Inst
WT308		Canberra B(I).6	Stored
XD860		Valiant BK.1	Nose
XE587		Hunter F.6	Stored
XF274		Meteor T.7	Remains
XF844		Provost T.1	Inst
XG158	8686M	Hunter F.6A	Fuselage
XJ396		Whirlwind HAR.10	Wreck
XM330		Wessex HAS.1	Inst
XN453	G-AMXD	Comet 2E	Sectioned
XN688	8141M	Sea Vixen FAW.2	Fire
XP166	G-APVL	Scout AH.1	Stored
XP393		Whirlwind HAR.10	Wreck
XP516	8580M	Gnat T.1	Inst
XP532	8615M	Gnat T.1	Wreck
XS482		Wessex HU.5	Inst
XT272		Buccaneer S.2	Dismantled
XV147		Nimrod proto	Sectioned
XV631		Wasp HAS.1	-
XW566		Jaguar B.08	Grounded
XX907		Lynx AH.1	Stored
XX910		Lynx HAS.2	Stored
		TSR-2	Nose

Locally

HB-NBA		Pup 150	ATC unit

FLEETLANDS
Royal Navy Aircraft Yard

XL600		Hunter T.7	Inst
XM836		Wessex HAS.3	Inst
XP110		Wessex HAS.3	
XS568		Wasp HAS.1	Inst
XS569		Wasp HAS.1	Inst
XS868	A2706	Wessex HAS.1	Gate
XS888		Wessex HAS.1	Travelling recruiting airframe
XT780		Wasp HAS.1	Inst

HAMBLE
Antique Aeroplane Company

G-ABDX		DH.60G Moth	Stored
G-ADGP		Hawk Speed Six	Restn
G-AFSW		Chilton DW.2	Stored
G-AISX		J-3C-65 Cub	Composite
G-BABA		Tiger Moth	Spares

C-7	G-ACFM	Avro Cadet	Stored

British Aerospace

XM693	7891M	Gnat T.1	Gate

HAVANT
Military Vehicle Conservation Group
Contact : 86 Priorsdean Crescent, Leigh Park, Havant, Hants, TO9 3AU.

G-AGYL		J/1 Autocrat	Restn

HEDGE END
(Off the A334 east of Southampton)
British Classic Aircraft Restorations
Contact : BCAR, 15 Steeple Close, Eastleigh, Hants, SO5 3AA.

G-AJEB		Auster J/1N	Frame
G-AJGJ	RT486	Auster 5	Restn
G-ANLU	TW448	Auster 5	Restn
G-ARDX		Auster 6A	Frame

HOOK
(North of the M3, near Junction 5)

G-AJXC		Auster 5	Restn

LASHAM
Dan-Air

G-AMSU"G-AMPP	Dakota IV	'Gate'

Royal Aerospace Establishment

G-ALYX		Comet 1	Noseless fuselage

Second World War Aircraft Preservation Society Open every weekend, except for Christmas. Contact : SWWAPS, Lasham Airfield, Alton, Hants.

G-APIT	VR192	Prentice 1	-
VH-FDT"G-APXX		Drover II	-
4X-FNA	WM366	Meteor NF.13	Composite with TT.20 WM234
WF137		Sea Prince C.1	-
WH291		Meteor F.8	-
XM833		Wessex HAS.3	-
WV798	A2557	Sea Hawk FGA.6	-
XE856		Vampire T.11	-
XK418	7976M	Auster AOP.9	-
XN309	A2663	Whirlwind HAR.9	-
XP360		Whirlwind HAR.10	-
E-423	G-9-444	Hunter F.51	-
2235		F-104G Starfighter	-

LEE-ON-SOLENT
HMS 'Daedalus' AES = Air Engineering School

EZ407		Harvard III	Preserved
NF389		Swordfish III	Preserved
VR930	8382M	Sea Fury FB.11	Preserved
WV382		Hunter GA.11	For sale
WV903	A2632	Sea Hawk FGA.4	AES
WV911	A2526	Sea Hawk FGA.6	AES 'flag-ship'

XE339	A2635	Sea Hawk FGA.6	AES
XG888		Gannet T.5	Stored
XL500	A2701	Gannet AEW.3	Stored
XL880	A2714	Whirlwind HAR.9	BDRT
XM843	A2693	Wessex HAS.1	AES
XM868		Wessex HAS.1	AES
XM874	A2689	Wessex HAS.1	AES
XM917	A2692	Wessex HAS.1	Fire
XN359	A2712	Whirlwind HAR.9	BDRT
XP150		Wessex HAS.3	AES
XP151	A2684	Wessex HAS.1	Fire
XP157	A2680	Wessex HAS.1	AES
XS483		Wessex HU.5	AES
XS496		Wessex HU.5	AES
XS507		Wessex HU.5	AES
XS508		Wessex HU.5	AES
XS510		Wessex HU.5	AES
XS511		Wessex HU.5	AES
XS513		Wessex HU.5	BDR
XS514		Wessex HU.5	AES
XS515		Wessex HU.5	AES
XS516		Wessex HU.5	AES
XS520		Wessex HU.5	AES
XS522		Wessex HU.5	AES
XS529		Wasp HAS.1	AES
XS538	A2725	Wasp HAS.1	BDRT
XS539		Wasp HAS.1	AES
XS545	A2702	Wasp HAS.1	BDRT
XS567		Wasp HAS.1	Inst
XS570	A2699	Wasp HAS.1	AES
XS862		Wessex HAS.3	AES
XS865	A2694	Wessex HAS.1	Fire
XS870	A2697	Wessex HAS.1	BDR
XS878	A2683	Wessex HAS.1	AES
XT429		Wasp HAS.1	AES
XT434		Wasp HAS.1	AES
XT449		Wessex HU.5	AES
XT453		Wessex HU.5	AES
XT455		Wessex HU.5	AES
XT482		Wessex HU.5	AES
XT484		Wessex HU.5	AES
XT485		Wessex HU.5	AES
XT487	A2723	Wessex HU.5	Fire
XT752	G-APYO	Gannet T.5	Stored
XT761		Wessex HU.5	AES
XT765		Wessex HU.5	AES
XT771		Wessex HU.5	AES
XT795		Wasp HAS.1	Gate
XV644	A2664	Sea King HAS.1	AES
		Lynx TA	AES
		Lynx TA	AES

L O W E R   U P H A M
(On the A333 near Bishop's Waltham)

G-AHUF	Tiger Moth	Restn
G-BILA	DM-165L Viking	Stored

M I D D L E   W A L L O P
Museum of Army Flying The Museum is
open 1000 to 1630 including weekends
and holidays. Contact : Museum of
Army Flying, Middle Wallop,
Stockbridge, Hampshire, SO20 8DY.
Telephone 0264 62121 extension 428.

G-APWZ		Prospector EP.9	Spares
G-APXW		Prospector EP.9	Spares
G-ARDG		Prospector EP.9	Restn
G-AXKS		W-Bell 47G-4A	−
B-415"BAPC163		AFEE 10/42 replica	Loan
P-5	8381M	Rotachute III	Loan
BAPC.10		Hafner R-II	Loan
5984" BAPC112		DH.2 replica	−
N5195	G-ABOX	Sopwith Pup	Loan
DG590	G-ADMW	Hawk Major	Loan
LH208		Horsa I	Sections
TJ569	G-AKOW	Auster 5	−
TK777		Hamilcar I	Sections
TL659	BAPC 80	Horsa II	Fuselage
VF516	G-ASMZ	Terrier 2	Restn
WJ358	G-ARYD	Auster AOP.6	−
WZ721		Auster AOP.9	−
XG502		Sycamore HR.14	−
XK776		ML Utility Mk 1	−
XK988	A2646	Whirlwind HAR.10	Stored
XL813		Skeeter AOP.12	−
XP821		Beaver AL.1	−
XP822		Beaver AL.1	−
XP847		Scout AH.1	−
XT108		Sioux AH.1	−
XT150		Sioux AH.1	Stored
XT190		Sioux AH.1	Stored
XT236		Sioux AH.1	Stored
XT548		Sioux AH.1	−
XT550		Sioux AH.1	Stored
XV272		Beaver AL.1	Cockpit, stored
		Belvedere HC.1	Cockpit
		Scout CIM	−
11989	N33600	L-19A Bird Dog	−
243809"BAPC185		WACO CG-4A	Fuselage
A-528	8769M	FMA Pucara	−
A-533	ZD486	FMA Pucara	−
AE-406		UH-1H Iroquois	−
AE-409		UH-1H Iroquois	−

Army Air Corps Historic Aircraft
Flight

XL814		Skeeter AOP.12	Airworthy
XP242		Auster AOP.9	Reserve
XR244		Auster AOP.9	Airworthy
XT131		Sioux AH.1	Airworthy

Air Engineering Training Wing (AETW)
and other airframes

WZ724	7432M	Auster AOP.9	Gate
XL847	A2626	Whirlwind HAS.7	Fire
XP191		Scout AH.1	BDRT
XP848		Scout AH.1	−
XP853		Scout AH.1	−
XP854	7898M	Scout AH.1	−
XP856		Scout AH.1	−
XP857		Scout AH.1	−

XP884	Scout AH.1	-
XP888	Scout AH.1	-
XP905	Scout AH.1	-
XP907	Scout AH.1	Fire
XR436	SARO P.531/2	BDRT
XR597	Scout AH.1	-
XR635	Scout AH.1	-
XT640	Scout AH.1	-
XV629	Wasp HAS.1	BDRT
XW836	Westland 606	-
XW838 TAD009	Lynx 1-03	-
XW888	Gazelle AH.1	-
XW889	Gazelle AH.1	-
XW900 TAD900	Gazelle AH.1	-
XW908	Gazelle AH.1	-
XW912	Gazelle AH.1	-
XX411	Gazelle AH.1	BDRT
XX452	Gazelle AH.1	Fire
XZ213 TAD213	Lynx AH.1	-
TAD.01	Gazelle CIM	-
TAD.02 WA22	Gazelle CIM	-
TAD.04	Gazelle CIM	-
TAD.08	Gazelle CIM	-
TAD.007 TO42	Lynx CIM	-
TAD.010	Lynx CIM	-
TAD.011	Lynx CIM	-
TAD.012	Lynx CIM	-
TAD.018	Lynx CIM	-
TAU.3 WA67	Gazelle CIM	-

O D I H A M

XK986	8790M	Whirlwind HAR.10	BDRT
XN387	8564M	Whirlwind HAR.9	BDRT
XP159	8877M	Wessex HAS.1	BDRT
XR453	8873M	Whirlwind HAR.10	Gate
XR681	8588M	Jet Provost T.4	Nose
		section, 1349 Sqn ATC	
XS871	8457M	Wessex HAS.1	Inst
		Scout AH.1	BDRT
61-2414		Boeing CH-47A	Inst

Locally

G-AMSC	SIPA 903	Stored
G-AWLG	SIPA 903	Stored

P O R T S M O U T H

John Pounds Yard

G-OARV	ARV Super 2	Stripped

S E A F I E L D   P A R K

XS869	A2649	Wessex HAS.1	Inst
		Buccaneer S.2	Nose

S O U T H A M P T O N

Southampton Hall of Aviation

The Museum is open daily except
Mondays and over the Christmas period,
1000 to 1700 (Tuesday to Saturday) and
1400 to 1700 (Sundays). Contact :
Southampton Hall of Aviation, Albert
Road South, Southampton, SO1 1FR.
Telephone 0703 635830. 424 Squadron,

ATC, also keep their aircraft with the
Museum. Both Museum and ATC have a
local store for some airframes.

G-ADWO	BB807	Tiger Moth	Stored
G-ALZE		BN-1F	Loan
BAPC.7		SUMPAC	-
		Airwave Hang-glider	-
VH-BRC VP-LVE		Sandringham 4	-
N248		Supermarine S.6A	-
PK683	7150M	Spitfire F.24	-
WA984		Meteor F.8	Stored
WK570	8211M	Chipmunk T.10	ATC, PAX
			trainer
WM571		Sea Venom FAW.22	Stored
XD596	7939M	Vampire T.11	ATC
XJ476		Sea Vixen FAW.1	Nose
			section, ATC
XJ481		Sea Vixen FAW.1	Stored
XK740	8396M	Gnat F.1	-
XL738	7860M	Skeeter AOP.12	-
XL853	A2630	Whirlwind HAS.7	Loan
XN246		Cadet TX.3	-
		Walrus/Seagull caravan,	
			Stored
		Gnat T.1	Nose

Crofton Aeroplane Services

G-AHHU		J/1N Alpha	Stored
G-APAA		J/5R Alpine	Stored
9M-ANN N70727		Chipmunk 22	Stored
18-1528		Super Cub	Stored

Others

G-ARLH		Terrier 1	Composite
G-BDMS		J-3C-65 Cub	Stored
WN411		Gannet AS.1	Nose
XD614	8124M	Vampire T.11	Nose

S O U T H A M P T O N   A I R P O R T

(Or Eastleigh)

XJ571	8140M	Sea Vixen FAW.2	Restn
XJ607	8171M	Sea Vixen FAW.2	Restn

T H R U X T O N

G-BCYY		W-Bell 47G-3B1	Wreck
G-BKZI		B.206B JetRanger	Wreck
G-ICRU		B.206A JetRanger	Wreck
	c/n 4463	Hiller UH-12E-4	Cabin
D-HEAS		AB.206B JetRanger	Wreck

W A R S A S H

(South of the A27 west of Fareham)

XM327	Wessex HAS.3	Inst

W H I T C H U R C H

G-AHWJ	LB294 T'craft Plus D	Restn

WINCHESTER

Charles Church (Spitfires) Ltd

G-CCIX	TE517	Spitfire IX	Restn
G-HUNN		Hispano Ha-1112	A/w
G-SUSY		P-51D-20-NA	Airworthy
EE606	G-MKVC	Spitfire V	Airworthy
MV262	G-CCVV	Spitfire XIV	Restn
PL344	G-IXCC	Spitfire IX	Restn
PT462	G-CTIX	Spitfire Tr IX	A/w
RR232		Spitfire IX	Restn
SM832	G-WWII	Spitfire XIV	Restn

Hereford & Worcester

DROITWICH

Rotorspan

G-AWRZ	Bell 47G-5	Wreck
G-BFVM	W-Bell 47G-3B1	Stored

EWYAS HAROLD

(On the A465 south west of Hereford)

G-AVYB	Trident 1E-140	Fuselage

FOWNHOPE

(On the B4224 south east of Hereford)

	Tiger Moth	Frame
	Tiger Moth	Frame

HEREFORD

RAF Hereford (Credenhill)

XE982	7564M	Vampire T.11	For tender
XG252	8840M	Hunter FGA.9	Gate

Others

K2572"	Tiger Moth replica	-

SHOBDON

G-AHHK		J/1 Autocrat	Restn
G-AJIT		Auster Kingsland	Restn
G-ANOR	G-ACDA	Tiger Moth	Composite
G-APSO		Dove 5	Stored
G-AVCT		Cessna F.150G	Restn
G-AWFF		Cessna F.150H	Restn
G-AXVC		Cessna FA.150K	Restn
G-AYFA		Twin Pioneer 3	Stored
G-BEPN		Pawnee 235D	Frame
G-BHAB		Cessna 152-II	Wreck
G-DHTM		Tiger Moth replica	-
N230ET	G-ATET	Twin Comanche 160	Stored

UPPER HILL

(Between the A4110 and the A49 south of Leominster) Lion Motors

WK275	Swift F.4	Displayed

Hertfordshire

BENINGTON

(South of the B1037 east of Stevenage)

EMK Aeroplane

G-AKHW		Gemini 1A	Restn
G-AOBG		Somers-Kendal SK.1	
			Stored
N5595T		C-47A-85-DL	Stored
S4523	N4727V	SPAD XIII	Restn

BERKHAMSTEAD

G-AVPD	Jodel D.9 Bebe	Stored
G-AWDW	Bensen CB-8M	Stored
G-AZZZ	Tiger Moth	Stored
G-BBGP	Berg Cricket	Stored

BISHOP'S STORTFORD

Russavia Collection, Woodend Green, Henham, Bishop's Stortford, Herts, CM22 6AY.

G-EBQP	Humming Bird	Stored
G-AKKH	Gemini 1A	Stored
BGA 162	Willow Wren	Stored
BGA 651	Slingsby Petrel	Restn
BGA 1147	Kranich II	Stored
BGA 2500	Fauvel AV-36CR	Stored

BUSHEY

VZ304	7630M	Vampire FB.5	Stored
		Venom FB.4	Pod
		Mystery Jet MJ-1	Mock-up

Breakers

G-BARI	Sundowner	Fuselage

CLOTHALL COMMON

(On the A507 south east of Baldock)

G-AIJS	Auster J/4	Stored
G-APYU	Tri-Traveler	Stored

ELSTREE

G-CHTT	Varga Kachina	Wreck

GOFF'S OAK

G-ATKG	Hiller UH-12B	Stored

H A T F I E L D
Polytechnic

	Jetstream	Fuselage

Locally
| G-AKXP | Auster 5 | Restn |

H A T F I E L D   A I R F I E L D
G-ACSS	DH.88 Comet	Airworthy
G-APLU	Tiger Moth	Restn
G-ARYB	HS.125 Srs 1	Inst
G-AWZO	Trident 3B-101	Inst
XS647	ATP (Andover)	Fuselage
236	G-AYBH HS.125-'800'	Fuselage
N14234	Jetstream '31'	Fuselage

H E M E L   H E M P S T E A D
| XK632 | Vampire T.11 | Pod, RAFA |

H I T C H I N
| G-BKEZ | PA-19-95 | Restn |

H O D D E S D O N
(On the A41 south of Ware) 1239 Squadron ATC
| XD616 | Vampire T.11 | - |

K I N G S   L A N G L E Y
(On the A41 north of Watford)
| XE327 | A2556 Sea Hawk FGA.6 | - |
| XJ494 | Sea Vixen FAW.2 | - |

L E A V E S D E N
G-AJPR	Dove 1B	Fuselage
WZ415	Vampire T.11	Pod, ATC
XR991	G-BOXO Gnat T.1	Restn

L E V E R S T O C K   G R E E N
(On the road between Abbotts Langley and Hemel Hempstead) The Swan at Pimlico
| WW442 | 7618M Provost T.1 | - |
| XL765 | Skeeter AOP.12 | - |

L O N D O N   C O L N E Y
(Off the A6 between London Colney and South Mimms) Mosquito Aircraft Museum
MAM is open from Easter to the end of October on Sundays and from July to the end of September on Thursday afternoons and is also open Bank Holidays. Groups are welcome at other times by prior arrangement. Opening times are Sunday 1030 to 1730 and Thursdays 1400 to 1730. Contact :

Mosquito Aircraft Museum, PO Box 107, Salisbury Hall, London Colney, near St Albans, Herts, AL2 1BU. Telephone 0727 22051 during Museum opening hours as outlined above.
G-ABLM	Cierva C.24	Loan
G-ADOT	Hornet Moth	-
G-ANFP	Tiger Moth	Fuselage
G-ANRX	Tiger Moth	Restn
G-AOJT	Comet 1XB	Fuselage
G-ARYC	HS.125 Srs 1	-
G-AVFH	Trident 2	Nose
BAPC 146	Toucan MPA	Centre body
BAPC 186	Queen Bee	Fuselage
D-IFSB	Dove 6	-
A1325	RAF BE.2e	Restn
W4050	Mosquito I	-
TA122	Mosquito FB.6	Fuselage
TA634	G-AWJV Mosquito TT.35	Restn
TJ118	Mosquito TT.35	Nose
TL615	Horsa II	Restn
WP790	G-BBNC Chipmunk T.10	-
WX853	7443M Venom NF.3	-
XE985	Vampire T.11	-
XG730	Sea Venom FAW.22	-
XJ565	Sea Vixen FAW.2	-
J-1008	Vampire FB.6	-

P A N S H A N G E R
G-ASOL	Bell 47D-1	Stored
G-BARJ	Bell 212	Wreck
G-BIJF	Bell 212	Wreck
G-BJYO	Tomahawk 115	Cockpit
LN-OQS	G-GLEN Bell 212	Stored
N5052P	G-ATFS Comanche 180	Stored
XT148	Sioux AH.1	Stored
XT803	Sioux AH.1	Stored
U-708	B.206 JetRanger	Stored

P A T M O R E
(North west of Bishop's Stortford)
| G-AYDJ | Cricket | Stored |

P O T T E R S   B A R
| G-AGYH | J/1N Alpha | Restn |
| F-BNZM | Wassmer D.120A | Restn |

R A B L E Y   H E A T H
(Off the A1M south of Stevenage)
| XP241 | Auster AOP.9 | - |

R O Y S T O N
G-ASBY	Airedale	Restn
G-BKXP	VT987 Auster AOP.6	Restn
A-20	VT984 Auster AOP.6	Spares

RUSH GREEN			
G-AEML	Dragon Rapide	Restn	
G-AYDV	Swalesong SA.II	Stored	
	Pawnee	Frame	
WT899	Cadet TX.3	Stored	

ST ALBANS
College of Further Education

WZ584	Vampire T.11	Inst
XE956	Vampire T.11	Inst
XH313	Vampire T.11	Inst

Humberside

BEVERLEY
Museum of Army Transport   Flemingate,
North Humberside. (0482 860445) Open
every day (except Xmas), 1000-1700.

XB259	G-AOAI	Beverley C.1	-
XP772		Beaver AL.1	-

BILTON

G-ANEJ	Tiger Moth	Stored

BREIGHTON

G-AIXN	M.1C Sokol	Restn
G-ATKY	Cessna 150F	Stored
G-BAOT	Rallye Club	Fuselage
G-BBWZ	AA-1B Trainer	Stored
G-JULY	AA-5A Cheetah	Fuselage
T9738	G-AKAT Magister	Restn

Locally

G-AHNH	Bestmann	Restn
G-AMYA	Bestmann	Restn
G-BOPY	Elster B	Restn

BROUGH

XN982	Buccaneer S.2C	Test rig
XT858	Phantom FG.1	Test rig
E-427 G-9-447	Hunter F.51	Inst

HULL
Specialised Spares

WL627	8488M	Varsity T.1	Stored
WP314	8634M	Sea Prince T.1	Stored

HUMBERSIDE AIRPORT
(Or Kirmington)

G-AJAE	J/1N Alpha	Restn

LACEBY

XR770	Lightning F.6	Stored
XS457	Lightning T.5	Nose
2257	F-104G	Stored

STORWOOD
(South east of York)

WH991	Dragonfly HR.3	Stored
WP503	Dragonfly HR.3	Stored
XP345	8792M Whirlwind HAR.10	Stored

Isle of Man

ISLE OF MAN AIRPORT
(Or Ronaldsway)

G-ACLL	Leopard Moth	Stored
G-AFFD	Percival Q.6	Restn
G-APSZ	Cessna 172	Stored

G-AROD	Cessna 175B	Wreck
G-AYVV	ST-10 Diplomate	Wreck
G-BAEO	Cessna F.172M	Fuselage
G-BCGA	Seneca 200	Wreck
	Stits Playboy	Frame

Isle of Wight

BEMBRIDGE
Pilatus Britten Norman

G-BJOG		BN-2 Islander	Stored
	c/n 917	BN-2 Islander	Stored
	c/n 920	BN-2 Islander	Stored
	c/n 2036	BN-2 Islander	Stored
	c/n 2041	BN-2 Islander	Stored

NEWPORT
Locally

G-AZJE	JB.01 Minicab	Stored
G-BCMF	Levi Go-Plane	Stored

S A N D O W N

G-AYTD	Aztec 250C	Fire			ARV Super 2	Test rig
G-BMWI	ARV Super 2	Fire	TE184	G-MXVI	Spitfire XVI	Restn
			5481		Hurricane	Rest

Kent

A S H F O R D

G-ANFY	Jackaroo	Restn

B R E D H U R S T
(South of Junction 4 of the M2, south of Gillingham)

G-BAXV	Cessna F.150L	Wreck
G-BEZA	Zlin Z.226T	Stored
G-BLAL	Cessna F.150L	Wreck

B R E N Z E T T
(On the A2070 north west of New Romney) Brenzett Aeronautical Museum The museum is open Sundays and Bank Holidays from Easter to October 1100 to 1700 and additionally Tuesdays, Wednesdays and Thursdays July to August from 1400 to 1700. Contact : Brenzett Aeronautical Museum, Ivychurch Road, Brenzett, Romney Marsh, Kent TN29 0EE.

G-AGPG	Avro XIX Srs 2	Stored
G-AMSM	Dakota 4	Nose
V7350	Hurricane I	Cockpit
WH657	Canberra B.2	-

C H A L L O C K   L E E S
(On the A251 north of Ashford)

G-AGYK	J/1 Autocrat	Restn
G-BCRH	Baldo 75	Stored

C H A T H A M
Royal Engineers Museum The museum is open Tuesday to Friday and Bank Holidays 1000 to 1700 and Sundays 1130 to 1700. Contact : Curator, Royal Engineers Museum, Brompton Barracks, Chatham, Kent ME4 4UG. Telephone 0634 44555 ext 2312.

XT133	7923M Sioux AH.1	Stored

Others

G-AXDB	J-3C-65 Cub	Stored
G-AYVP	Woody Pusher	Stored
G-BCNC	GY-201 Minicab	Restn
WZ846	8439M Chipmunk T.10	1404 Sqn, ATC, Boundary Road

C H A T T E N D O N
(On the A228 north of Rochester) Defence Explosive Ordnance Disposal School

BAPC 158	Fieseler Fi 103 (V1)	Gate
BAPC 159	Yokosuka Ohka II	Gate
WT301	Canberra B.6(mod)	Gate

C H I S L E T
(North of the A28 south of Herne Bay)

G-ANOR	Tiger Moth	Restn

H A W K I N G E
(On the A260 north of Folkestone) Kent Battle of Britain Museum The museum is open Sundays and all Bank Holidays Easter to the end of October 1100 to 1700 and from May to the end of September Monday to Saturday 1100 to 1700. Contact : Kent Battle of Britain Museum, c/o Little Milton, Pay Street, Hawkinge, Kent.

BAPC 36	Fi 103 (V1) replica	-
N3289"BAPC65	Spitfire replica	-
P3059"BAPC64	Hurricane replica	-
XP701 8924M	Lightning F.3	-
1480" BAPC66	'Bf 109' replica	-

H E A D C O R N
(Or Lashenden) Lashenden Air Warfare Museum LAWM is open Sundays and Bank Holidays 1030 to 1800 from Easter until the end of October. Parties are welcome at other times by prior arrangement. Contact : LAWM, Headcorn Airfield, Ashford, Kent TN27 9HX. Telephone 0622 890226.

BAPC 91	Fi 103R-IV	-
WZ589	Vampire T.11	-
XN380	Whirlwind HAS.7	-
84	Mystere IVA	Loan
63938	F-100F-16-NA	

Airfield

G-AHAV	J/1 Autocrat	Stored
G-AJRE	J/1 Autocrat	Restn
G-ANHZ	Auster 5	Restn

L Y M P N E

BAPC 79	Fiat G.46-IV	Stored

M A I D S T O N E

G-ARRL	J/1N Alpha	Restn
G-AYYL	T.61A Falke	Restn

M A N S T O N

Memorial Building and Gate Guardians

BN230"	LF751	Hurricane II	-
TB752	8086M	Spitfire XVI	-
WE168	8049M	Canberra PR.3	-
XH764	7972M	Javelin FAW.9	-

RAF Fire Services Central Training Establishment

G-BDRC		Viscount 724	Poor
VP953		Devon C.2/2	Poor
VP956		Devon C.2/2	-
VP963		Devon C.2/2	Composite
VP965	8823M	Devon C.2/2	-
XD527		Vampire T.11	Poor
XG327	8188M	Lightning F.1	-
XH590		Victor K.1A	Poor
XH616		Victor K.1A	Poor
XJ430		Whirlwind HAR.10	-
XJ695	8738M	Hunter FGA.9	-
XK968	8445M	Whirlwind HAR.10	-
XK969	8646M	Whirlwind HAR.10	Poor
XL386	8760M	Vulcan B.2A	-
XM657	8734M	Vulcan B.2A	-
XN602	8088M	Jet Provost T.3	-
XN855	8556M	Argosy E.1	-
XP333	8650M	Whirlwind HAR.10	-
XP357	8499M	Whirlwind HAR.10	-
XP394		Whirlwind HAR.10	-
XP400	8444M	Whirlwind HAR.10	Poor
XP741	8939M	Lightning F.3	-
ZD233	G-ASGE	Super VC-10	Fuselage

R O C H E S T E R

G-BJHS	Sunderland V	Restn

R O C H E S T E R   A I R P O R T

Medway Aircraft Preservation Society

The workshop facilities are open to the public on Sunday mornings and Monday evenings, but Airport rules must be observed. Contact : R T Twine, c/o GEC Avionics, Airport Works, Rochester, Kent. Telephone 0634 44400.

LF738	5405M	Hurricane II	Stored
PL965		Spitfire PR.XI	Restn
MM54099		T-6G Texan	Restn
6771"	FU-6	F-84F-51-RE	-

Airfield

N96240	Beech D.18S (3TM)	Stored

S E V E N O A K S

Biggin Hill Air Museum and Friends of Biggin Hill

Contact : Peter Smith, Curator, 34, Derry Downs, St Mary Cray, Kent BR5 4DU.

G-AAXK		Klemm L-25.1A	Fuselage
G-BAYV		Noralpha	-
K5054"	B'190	Spitfire replica	-
WP250		Vampire NF.10	Pod
XD535		Vampire T.11	-
		Typhoon IA	Cockpit
		Chipmunk T.10	Cockpit

Locally

G-APJZ	J/1N Alpha	Restn
G-AWGA	Airedale	Stored

S H O R N C L I F F E

(Near Lydd) Sir John Moore Barracks

Wessex HC.2	Inst

S M E E T H

(On the A20 between Ashford and Sellinge)

G-ASER	Aztec 250B	Wreck

T U N B R I D G E   W E L L S

G-ANOD	Tiger Moth	Stored
G-APJO	Tiger Moth	Wreck
G-ISIS	Tiger Moth	Wreck

Lancashire

B A C U P

Pennine Aviation Museum

Contact : David Stansfield, School House, Sharneyford, Bacup, Lancashire OL13 9UQ. Telephone 0706 875967.

G-ARHT	Caribbean 150	Frame
BAPC 157	CG-4A Hadrian	Frame
VV901	Anson T.21	-
WF911	Canberra B.2	Nose
WJ721	Canberra TT.18	-
WN149	Balliol T.2	Nose
WN534	Balliol T.2	Nose
XG297	Hunter FGA.9	Nose
XK627	Vampire T.11	-
	AW Albemarle	Nose

B L A C K B U R N

1262 Squadron ATC, Preston Old Road

Chipmunk T.10	PAX tnr

BLACKPOOL AIRPORT
(Or Squires Gate)

G-ASXR	Cessna 210	Restn
G-ATRS	Cherokee 140	Stored
G-AVPH	Cessna F.150G	Wreck
G-AXSX	Sundowner	Wreck
F-BHMU G-BHVZ	Cessna 180	Restn
F-BMGR G-BHTC	CEA DR.1051/M1	Restn
XL391	Vulcan B.2A	Static

COCKERHAM
(Or Banks End, on the A588 between Lancaster and Fleetwood)

G-ARZE	Cessna 172C	Para-tnr

ECCLESTONE
(On the B5250 south of Leyland) Bygone Times Antique Warehouse Open daily.

BAPC 28	Wright Flyer rep	-
E373" BAPC178	Avro 504K replica	-
	CASA 2-111	Nose

HEYSHAM
Helicopter Museum of Great Britain
Contact : Jim Wilkie, 'Wavecrest', 4 Rydal Road, Morecambe, LA3 1DT. Telephone 0524 413253.

G-AWRP	Grasshopper III	-
G-AXFM	Grasshopper III	Rig
G-AZAU	Grasshopper III	Rig
5X-UUW	Scout	Wreck
XK482 G-BJWC	Skeeter AOP.10	-
XK940 G-AYXT	Whirlwind HAS.7	-
XN386 A2713	Whirlwind HAR.9	-
XX469 G-BNCL	Lynx 1-07	-
130191 G-BJWY	Whirlwind HAR.21	-

LANCASTER
Lancashire Fire Brigade HQ

RG-05	Lynx static rig	Inst

RAMSGREAVE
(Between the A59 and the A6119 north of Blackburn)

WG751	Dragonfly HR.3	-

SAMLESBURY
WT537	Canberra PR.7	Gate

WARTON
WJ857		Canberra T.4	Nose
XN973		Buccaneer S.1	Nose
XX736	G27-327	Jaguar GR.1	Stored
XX765		Jaguar GR.1(mod)	Stored
ZF577	53-668	Lightning F.53	Stored
ZF579	53-671	Lightning F.53	Stored
ZF580	53-672	Lightning F.53	Stored
ZF581	53-675	Lightning F.53	Stored
ZF582	53-676	Lightning F.53	Stored
ZF584	53-682	Lightning F.53	Stored
ZF585	53-683	Lightning F.53	Stored
ZF586	53-688	Lightning F.53	Stored
ZF587	53-691	Lightning F.53	Stored
ZF589	53-700	Lightning F.53	Stored
ZF590	53-679	Lightning F.53	Stored
ZF591	53-685	Lightning F.53	Stored
ZF592	53-686	Lightning F.53	Stored
ZF593	53-692	Lightning F.53	Stored
ZF595	55-714	Lightning T.55	Stored
ZF596	55-715	Lightning T.55	Stored
ZF597	55-711	Lightning T.55	Stored
	AV.023	Tornado ADV	Test rig
		Strikemaster	Inst
Q497	G27-116	Canberra T.4	Dump

Leicestershire

BRUNTINGTHORPE
XR728	Lightning F.6	Static
85	Mystere IVA	'Gate'

COTTESMORE
WH791	8187M	Canberra PR.7	Gate
XJ582	8139M	Sea Vixen FAW.2	Fire
XL618	8892M	Hunter T.7	BDRT
XM656	8757M	Vulcan B.2A	Nose
XR716	8940M	Lightning F.3	Fire

EARL SHILTON
(On the A47 north east of Hinckley)

G-AMUI	J/5F Aiglet Tr	Stored

EAST MIDLANDS AIRPORT
East Midlands Aeropark Visitors Centre
The centre is still open daily from 1000. Closing times vary with the time of year. Contact : East Midlands Airport Aeropark, Castle Donington, Derby DE7 2SA. Telephone 0332 810621.

G-BEOZ	Argosy 101	-
G-FRJB	SA.1 Sheriff	-
VR-BEP G-BAMH	Whirlwind Srs 3	-
WL626 G-BHDD	Varsity T.1	-
XM575 G-BLMC	Vulcan B.2A	-
ZF588 53-693	Lightning F.53	-

Airport Site

G-APEG	Merchantman	Fire
G-APES	Merchantman	Stored
G-AZLR	Viscount 813	Cabin tnr
G-BKTJ	Cessna 404 Titan	Wreck

H U S B A N D S   B O S W O R T H

G-AWIF	Mosquito gyro	Stored

L E I C E S T E R

Leicester   Museum   of   Technology

Contact   :   Peter   Stoddart, Leicestershire Museums, 96 New Walk, Leicester LE1 6TD.   Telephone 0533 765532.   The Museum itself is open Monday to Saturday 1000 to 1730 and Sundays 1400 to 1730.

G-AIJK	Auster J/4	Restn
G-AJRH	J/1N Alpha	Stored
XP280	Auster AOP.9	Stored

L E I C E S T E R   A I R P O R T

(Or Leicester East)

G-AEXZ		J/2 Cub	Restn
G-AFTN		T'craft Plus C2	Restn
G-AGOH		J/1 Autocrat	Airworthy
G-AGVG		J/1 Autocrat	Stored
G-APMH		J/1U Workmaster	Restn
NJ695	G-AJXV	Auster IV	Restn
XK417	G-AVXY	Auster AOP.9	Restn

L O U G H B O R O U G H

G-AOBU	Jet Provost 1	Inst

L U T T E R W O R T H

Area

G-AGWE		Avro XIX Srs 2	Stored
G-AXCI		Bensen B.8M	Stored
XM426"		Jet Provost T.4	Nose
E-407	G-9-435	Hunter F.51	Stored

M A R K E T   H A R B O R O U G H

Kibworth Aviation Group

WZ608	Vampire T.11	-

N O R T H   L U F F E N H A M

WS776	7716M	Meteor NF.14	Gate
XG194	8839M	Hunter FGA.9	BDRT
XJ608	8802M	Sea Vixen FAW.2	BDRT
XN699	8224M	Sea Vixen FAW.2	Inst
XP344	8764M	Whirlwind HAR.10	Inst
XP921	8226M	Sea Vixen FAW.2	BDRT

S T A N F O R D

(Off the B5414 north east of Rugby) Stanford Hall Motorcycle Museum/Percy Pilcher Display Open Easter to end of September, Thurs, Sat, Sun and Bank Holidays, 1430-1800. (0788 860250)

BAPC 45	Pilcher Hawk rep	-

Lincolnshire

B O S T O N

G-AWUB	Gardan GY-201	Stored
G-BDBV	Aero Jodel D.11A	Stored
G-BFDM	Wassmer D.120	Fuselage
G-BGEW	SNCAN NC.854S	Restn
G-BIOI	SAN DR.1051M	Stored
F-BBGH	Brochet MB.100	Stored
F-PFUG	Adam RA-14	Stored

B O S T O N   A I R F I E L D

(Or Wyberton)

G-ASFZ		Pawnee 235	Frame
G-BGPO		Pawnee 235D	Frame
NJ673	G-AOCR	Auster 5D	Stored

C A S T L E   B Y T H A M

(East of the A1, north of Stamford)

F-BBBN	J-3C-65 Cub	Spares

C O N I N G S B Y

Battle   of   Britain   Memorial   Flight Open Monday to Friday (except Bank Holidays) 1000 to 1700 - the last guided tour taking place at 15.30.

Booking is not required, but is advisable.   Please note that the aircraft of the Flight may not all be present as they may well be positioning back from or to a display. Contact : BBMF Visits, RAF Coningsby, Lincoln LN4 4SY. Tel : 0526 44041.

P7350	G-AWIJ	Spitfire IIA	-
AB910	G-AISU	Spitfire VB	-
LF363		Hurricane IIC	-
PA474		Lancaster I	-
PM631		Spitfire PR.XIX	-
PS853		Spitfire PR.XIX	Restn
PS915	7711M	Spitfire PR.XIX	-
PZ865	G-AMAU	Hurricane IIC	-
VP981		Devon C.2/2	-
WK518		Chipmunk T.10	-

Others

WJ815	8729M	Canberra PR.7	Fire
XM987		Lightning T.4	Fire
XN774	8551M	Lightning F.2A	Decoy
XW528	8861M	Buccaneer S.2B	BDR

CRANWELL

WH699"	WJ637	Canberra B.2	Gate
XD429"	XD542	Vampire T.11	Gate
XF375	8736M	Hunter F.6	Inst
XF516	8685M	Hunter F.6A	Inst
XG209	8709M	Hunter F.6	Inst
XJ634	8684M	Hunter F.6A	Inst
XJ639	8687M	Hunter F.6A	Inst
XK149	8714M	Hunter F.6A	Inst
XL577	8676M	Hunter T.7	Inst
XN643	8704M	Jet Provost T.3	Nose
XX821	8896M	Jaguar GR.1	Inst

DIGBY

WH166	8052M	Meteor T.7	Gate

EAST KIRKBY

Lincolnshire Aviation Heritage Centre

G-ADFV	2893M	Blackburn B-2	Nose
G-AJOZ	FK338	Argus II	Restn
G-AXEI		Ward Gnome	-
G-BBUW		SA.102 Cavalier	Fuse
G-BEEX		Comet 4C	Nose
BGA 794		T.8 Tutor	Stored
BAPC 43		Mignet HM.14	-
BAPC 61		Stewart Ornithopter	-
BAPC 101		Mignet HM.14	Fuselage
BAPC 154		D.31 Turbulent	Fuselage
		Knight Twister	Frame
AE436		Hampden I	Remains
NP294		Proctor IV	-
NX611	G-ASXX	Lancaster VII	-
VV119	7285M	Supermarine 535	Cockpit
WD954		Canberra B.2	Nose
WW421	7688M	Provost T.1	-
XA909		Vulcan B.1	Nose
XE677		Hunter F.4	-
XH670		Victor B.2/BS	Nose
XM561	7980M	Skeeter AOP.12	-
100502		Fa 330A-1	-

FENLAND

(Or Holbeach St Johns)

G-AREL	Caribbean 150	Restn
G-ASTV	Cessna 150D	Restn
G-AWAX	Cessna 150D	Spares
G-LOOK	Cessna F.172M	Cockpit

HEMSWELL

Hemswell Aviation Society Museum open on a limited basis, contact : 75 Sixhill Street, Grimsby, South Humberside, DN32 9HS

G-EASQ"BAPC87	Bristol Babe replica	-
G-AEJZ B'120	Mignet HM.14	-
G-AFFI"BAPC77	Mignet HM.14	-
BAPC 161	Stewart Ornithopter	-
WH796	Canberra PR.7	Nose
WH946 8185M	Canberra B.6(mod)	Fuse
WJ975	Canberra T.19	

XD445		Vampire T.11	-
XG195/WT741		Hunter FGA.9/GA.11	Composite
XG506	7852M	Sycamore HR.14	-
		Wessex HAS.1	Nose
101		Mystere IVA	-

ROPSLEY

(South of the A52 between Grantham and Boston)

G-ARKG	J/5G Autocar	Restn
G-BFBN	Pawnee 235D	Frame

SCAMPTON

VZ467		Meteor F.8	Stored
XE653	8829M	Hunter F.6A	Inst
XE920	8196M	Vampire T.11	Stored
XF515	8830M	Hunter F.6A	Inst
XG160	8831M	Hunter F.6A	Inst
XG172	8832M	Hunter F.6A	Inst
XL587	8807M	Hunter T.7	Inst
XL592	8836M	Hunter T.7	Inst
XR571	8493M	Gnat T.1	Gate

SKEGNESS

(Or Ingoldmells)

G-AHAL	J/1N Alpha	Spares

STRUBBY

XP706	8925M	Lightning F.3	Static

STURGATE

G-BCTF	Warrior 151	Restn
G-BEYS	Cherokee 180	Restn
G-BFXZ	Archer II	Wreck
	Cessna	Para-tnr

SUTTON BRIDGE

(On the A17 west of King's Lynn)

G-ASTG	Nord 1002	Stored
G-ASUA	Nord 1002	Stored

SWINDERBY

WG362	8630M	Chipmunk T.10	PAX tnr
WT520	8184M	Canberra PR.7	Gate
XD506	7983M	Vampire T.11	Gate
XG329	8050M	Lightning F.1	Displayed

TATTERSHALL THORPE

G-AEOH	Mignet HM.14	Stored
G-APMP	Hiller UH-12C	Stored
G-ASKJ	Terrier 1	Wreck
G-ATHF	Cessna 150F	Wreck
G-ATJU	Cessna 150F	Wreck
G-AVVE	Cessna F.150H	Wreck
G-AWCL	Cessna F.150H	Wreck
G-AXGA	PA-18-95 Super Cub	Wreck
G-AXRC	Cricket	Stored
G-AYFY	EAA Biplane	Frame
G-AYJW	Cessna FR.172G	Wreck

Reg		Type	Status
G-AYVT		Brochet MB.84	Wreck
G-AZVV		Cherokee 180G	Wreck
G-AZYJ		Wilga 35	Wreck
G-BAYX		Bell 47G-5	Wreck
G-BCRA		Cessna F.150M	Wreck
G-BDID		Chipmunk 22	Wreck
G-BDJG		Luton Minor	Wreck
G-BDNE		Harker Hawk	Unfinished
G-BEYM		Cessna F.150M	Wreck
G-BFGA		Rallye 150ST	Wreck
G-BFMS		Rallye 180GT	Wreck
G-BFMT		Robin HR200/100	Wreck
G-BFON		Turbo Navajo	Wreck
G-BGHA		Cessna F.152	Wreck
G-BGNS		Cessna F.172N	Wreck
G-BGRJ		Cessna T.310R	Wreck
G-BGZE		Tomahawk 112	Wreck
G-BGZH		Tomahawk 112	Wreck
G-BHOC		Commander 112A	Wreck
G-BISK		Commander 112A	Wreck
G-BJCY		Slingsby T.67A	Wreck
G-BKAB		ICA IS-28M2A	Wreck
G-BKVM		Super Cub 150	Wreck
G-BLSS		Cessna F.150J	Wreck
G-BMWM		ARV Super 2	Wreck
G-HASL		AA-5A Cheetah	Wreck
G-HSKY		Hughes H.369HM	Wreck
G-LINT		Pitts S-1S	Wreck
G-OADE		Cessna F.177RG	Wreck
G-PULL		Super Cub 150	Wreck
C-GOEA	G-BMSP	Hughes 369HS	Restn
D-ECIU		Cessna F.172H	Wreck
EI-BKL		Cessna FR.172F	Wreck
5X-UUX	G-BKLJ	Scout	Spares
WV703	G-IIIM"	Pembroke C.1	Wreck
XL735		Skeeter AOP.12	Stored
XP329	8791M	Whirlwind HAR.10	Stored
XP395	8674M	Whirlwind HAR.10	Stored
XT788	G-BMIR	Wasp HAS.1	Restn

WADDINGTON

Reg		Type	Status
XH558		Vulcan B.2A	Airworthy
XJ825	8810M	Vulcan K.2	BDR
XL189	8912M	Victor K.2	Gate
XM607	8779M	Vulcan B.2A	Gate

WICKENBY

Reg	Type	Status
G-AIGM	J/1N Alpha	Poor shape
G-AIPV	J/1 Autocrat	Stored
G-ARLK	Comanche 250	Restn
G-BEYS	Archer II	Spares
G-DCAT	Turbo AgCat	Spares
G-ROAN	Stearman B75N-1	Wreck

Greater London

BENTLEY PRIORY

Reg		Type	Status
		Spitfire replica	Gate
XG290	8711M	Hunter F.6	Gate
XM173	8414M	Lightning F.1A	Gate

BIGGIN HILL

Reg		Type	Status
NP181	G-AOAR	Proctor IV	Stored

BIGGIN HILL AIRPORT

RAF Memorial Chapel

Reg		Type	Status
		Hurricane replica	Gate
N3194"		Spitfire replica	Gate

Warbirds of Great Britain

Reg		Type	Status
G-SXVI	TE356	Spitfire XVI	Airworthy
NX55JP		F4U Corsair	Airworthy
N179NP		F4U-5 Corsair	Airworthy
NL314BG		P-51D Mustang	Airworthy
NX49092		F4U-4 Corsair	Airworthy
N52113		P-63C Kingcobra	Restn
BR601		Spitfire IX	Stored
NH238	G-MKIX	Spitfire IX	Airworthy
PL983	G-PRXI	Spitfire PR.XI	Airworthy
PP972		Seafire III	Stored
PV260"	BR601	Spitfire IX	Stored
RW386	G-BXVI	Spitfire XVI	Stored
SM969	G-BRAF	Spitfire XVIII	Stored
TE392	7000M	Spitfire XVI	Stored
9663"		Bf 109G-10	Stored
T2-124		Bf 109K	Stored

Others

Reg	Type	Status
G-ABYA	DH.60G Moth	Stored
G-AKVZ	Messenger IVB	Restn
G-AOGE	Proctor III	Stored
G-AOKH	Prentice 1	Spares
G-APZR	Cessna 150	Engine rig
G-AREE	Aztec 250	Stored
G-ARWC	Cessna 150B	Wreck
G-ASDA	Queen Air 65-80	Stored
G-ASTP	Hiller UH-12C	Restn
G-AVWE	Cherokee 140	Stored
G-AWCO	Cessna F.150H	Fuselage
G-AWEK	Fournier RF-4D	Fuselage
G-AYRM	Cherokee 140D	Wreck
G-BEAC	Cherokee 140	Stored
G-BHYS	Cherokee 181	Wreck
No 7	Civilian Coupe	Spares
	Scout AH.1	Cockpit
	Hunter F.51/T.7	Gate

CHESSINGTON
(On the A243 south of Surbiton)

Reg	Type	Status
G-AWJX	Zlin Z.526	Restn
	Pitts S-1	Frame
	Pitts S-1	Frame

C O U L S D O N
(South Circular, south of Croydon)
G-ASDF   Edwards Gyro   Stored

E N F I E L D
WK587   8212M Chipmunk T.10   PAX tnr,
                                 College
XW922   8885M Harrier GR.3   BAe/ROF

H A M P T O N
G-ADNZ"   Tiger Moth   Stored

H A N W E L L
(On the A4020 east of Uxbridge)
G-AETG   Aeronca 100   Stored
G-AEWV   Aeronca 100   Stored
G-AEXD   Aeronca 100   Stored

H A N W O R T H
G-AWGM   Kittiwake II   Restn

H A Y E S
(On the A4020 south east of Uxbridge)
Science Museum Storage Facility
G-ATTN   Piccard HAB   Canopy
BAPC 52   Lilienthal Glider   -
               Gossamer Albatross MPA -

H E N D O N
Royal Air Force Museum Complex Open
1000-1800 Mon-Sat and 1400-1800 Sun.
Single entry charge for all three
sections.   Contact : RAF Museum,
Hendon, London NW9 5LL. (01 205 2266)
Battle of Britian Museum
K8042   8372M Gladiator II   -
L8756"   10001 Bolingbroke IVT   -
N1671   8370M Defiant I   -
P2617   8373M Hurricane I   -
P3175   Hurricane I   Wreck
R9125   8377M Lysander III   -
X4590   8384M Spitfire I   -
ML824   Sunderland V   -
A2-4   VH-ALB Seagull V   -
4101   8477M Bf 109E-3   -
360043   8475M Ju 88R-1   -
494083   8474M Ju 87D-3   -
701152   8471M He 111H-23   -
730301   8479M Bf 110G-4/R6   -
MM5701   8468M Fiat CR-42   -
Bomber Command Museum and United
States Army Air Force Memorial
168   G-BFDE Tabloid replica   -
F1010   DH.9A   -
F8614"   G-AWAU Vimy replica   -
R5868   7325M Lancaster I   -
W1048   8465M Halifax II   -
MF628   Wellington T.10   -
TW117   7805M Mosquito T.3   -
XD818   7894M Valiant BK.1   -

XL318   8733M Vulcan B.2A   -
429366   8838M TB-25N-20-NC Mitchell -
483868   B-17G-95-DL Fortress   -
Royal Air Force Museum of Aviation
History
G-EBMB   Hawker Cygnet   -
BAPC 82   Afghan Hind   -
BAPC 100   Clarke TWK   Loan
164   BAPC 106 Bleriot XI   -
433   BAPC 107 Bleriot XXVII   -
2345"   G-ATVP FB.5 Gunbus replica -
3066   G-AETA Caudron G.III   -
A301   Morane BB   Fuselage
E449"   Avro 504K   Composite
F938   G-EBIC RAF SE.5A   -
A8226"   G-BIDW 1½ Strutter replica -
E2466"   B'165 Bristol F.2b   -
F6314   Camel F.1   -
J9941"   G-ABMR Hart   -
K4232   Cierva C.30A   -
K9942   8383M Spitfire IA   -
N5182"   G-APUP Sopwith Pup replica -
N5628   Gladiator II   Fuselage
N5912   8385M Sopwith Triplane   -
T6296   8387M Tiger Moth II   -
Z7197   8380M Proctor III   -
KK995   Hoverfly I   -
MN235   Typhoon IB   -
NV778   8386M Tempest V   Composite
PK724   7288M Spitfire F.24   -
RD253   7931M Beaufighter TF.10   -
VT812   7200M Vampire F.3   -
VX653   Sea Fury FB.11   -
WE139   8369M Canberra PR.3   -
WH301   7930M Meteor F.8   -
WK281   7712M Swift FR.5   -
WP185   7583M Hunter F.5   -
XG474   8367M Belvedere HC.1   -
XH124   8025M Beverley C.1   -
XP831   8406M Hawker P.1127   -
XS925   Lightning F.6   -
               Beaufighter   Nose
920   Stranraer   -
A16-199 G-BEOX Hudson IIIA   -
HD-75   G-AFDX Hanriot HD.1   -
HD5-1   Dornier Do 24T-3   -

H O U N S L O W
Imperial War Museum store
TV959   Mosquito T.3   -

H O U N S L O W   H E A T H
Metropolitan Police Training Centre
G-AVFK   Trident 2E   Fuselage

K E N L E Y
VM791"   XA312 Cadet TX.3   135 Sqn ATC
                          Travelling airframe

K I N G S T O N - U P O N -
T H A M E S

| XW272 | Harrier T.2 | Nose, BAe |

L O N D O N   A I R P O R T
(Or Heathrow)

G-APDT	Comet 4	Fire
G-AVFG	Trident 2E	Inst
G-AWZK	Trident 3B-101	Inst

N O R T H O L T

| | Spitfire replica | Gate |

O R P I N G T O N
(On the A224 in south east London)

| G-AHLI | Auster 3 | Stored |

R U I S L I P

| WM729 | Vampire NF.10 | Pod |
| WZ581 | Vampire T.11 | - |

S O U T H   K E N S I N G T O N

The Science Museum   The Museum is open daily 1000 to 1800 and Sundays 1430 to 1800.   Contact, The Science Museum, South Kensington, London SW7 2DD. Telephone 01 938 8000.

G-EBIB	F939	RAF SE.5A	-
G-AAAH		DH.60G Moth	-
G-ANAV		Comet 1A	Nose
G-ATDD		Beagle 206-1	Nose
G-ATTN		Piccard HAB	Basket
G-BBGN		Cameron A-375	Gondola
G-9-185	N-250	Hunter F.6	Nose
BAPC	50	Roe No 1 Triplane	-
BAPC	51	Vickers Vimy IV	-
BAPC	53	Wright Flyer replica	-
BAPC	54	JAP-Harding Monoplane	-
BAPC	55	Antoinette 1909	-
BAPC	57	Pilcher Hawk replica	-
BAPC	124	Lilienthal replica	-
		Short Gas Balloon Basket	
		Airship No 17	Gondola
OO-BFH		Piccard Gas	Gondola
304	BAPC 62	Cody Biplane	-
D7560		Avro 504K	-
J8067		Pterodactyl 1	-
L1592		Hurricane I	-
P9444		Spitfire IA	-
S1595		Supermarine S.6B	-
W4041/G		Gloster E.28/39	-
AP507	G-ACWP	Cierva C.30A	-
EE416		Meteor III	Nose
KN448		Dakota IV	Nose
VX185	7631M	Canberra B.8	Nose
XN344	8018M	Skeeter AOP.12	-
XP505		Gnat T.1	-
210/16	BAPC56	Fokker E.III	-
100509		Fa 330A-1	Stored

| 191316 | | Me 163B-1a Komet | - |
| 442795 | BAPC199 | Fi 103 (V1) | - |

S O U T H   L A M B E T H

Imperial War Museum   The Museum is open 1000 to 1750 weekdays and 1400 to 1750 on Sundays.   Contact : Imperial War Museum, Lambeth Road, London SE1 6HZ.   Telephone : 01 735 8922.

BAPC 198	Fi 103 (V1)	-
2699	RAF BE.2c	-
N6812	Camel 2F1	-
R6915	Spitfire I	-
DV372	Lancaster I	Nose
733682	AM.75	Fw 190A-8	-
472258"	9246	P-51D Mustang	-
01120	MiG-15bis	-

S O U T H A L L
(On the A4020 south east of Uxbridge)
Technical College

G-AREF		Aztec 250	Inst
G-ARMN		Cessna 175B	Inst
G-MBTY		American Eagle	Inst
WB763	G-BBMR	Chipmunk T.10	Inst
XD536	7734M	Vampire T.11	Inst
XL763		Skeeter AOP.12	Inst
Others			
		Canberra	Nose

S T A I N E S

| VP-KKO | J/5G Autocar | Stored |

S T A N M O R E   P A R K
(On the A4140 in north west London)

| XA553 | 7470M | Javelin FAW.1 | Gate |

S U N B U R Y - O N - T H A M E S
Sunbury Salvage Company, Fordbridge Road.

| | Hobbycopter | Displayed |

U X B R I D G E

| | Spitfire replica | Gate |

W E L L I N G

| XN437 | G-AXWA | Auster AOP.9 | Stored |

W E S T   D R A Y T O N
(Off the A4/M4 north of London Airport)

| XN769 | 8402M | Lightning F.2 | Gate |

W O O L W I C H

Royal Artillery Institution, Old Royal Military Academy, Red Lion Lane, Woolwich, London SE18 4JJ. Telephone 01 854 5533 for visiting details.

| XR271 | Auster AOP.9 | - |

Greater Manchester

A L T R I N C H A M

XD595	Vampire T.11	Pod

A S H T O N - U N D E R - L Y N E

WP927	8216M	Chipmunk T.10	PAX tnr

B A R T O N   A E R O D R O M E

G-APVV	Mooney M.20A	Stored
G-AXWE	Cessna F.150K	Wreck
G-AYWD	Cessna 182N	Stored
G-BKPU	Broussard	Wreck

L E V E N S H U L M E
(On the A6 south east of Manchester)
1940 Squadron, ATC, St Oswalds Road

N6720	7014M	Tiger Moth	Fuselage

M A N C H E S T E R
Greater Manchester Museum of Science
and Industry   The Museum is open
every day from 1030 to 1700 including
Bank Holidays but excluding December
23-25.   Contact : Greater Manchester
Museum   of   Science   and   Industry,
Liverpool   Road,   Castlefield,
Manchester M3 4JP.   Tel 061 832 2244.

G-EBZM		Avian IIIA	Loan
G-ADAH		Dragon Rapide	Restn
G-APUD		Bensen B.7M	Loan
G-AWZP		Trident 3B-101	Nose
BAPC 6		Roe Triplane rep	Loan
BAPC 89		Cayley Glider replica	–
BAPC 98	8485M	Ohka II	–
BAPC175		Volmer VJ-23	–
BAPC182		Wood Ornithopter	Stored
H2311	G-ABAA	Avro 504K	Restn
T9707"	8378M	Magister I	–
BL614	4354M	Spitfire Vb	–
WB440		Firefly AS.6	Nose
WG763	7816M	EE P.1A	–
WP270	8598M	Eton TX.1	–
WR960	8772M	Shackleton AEW.2	–
WT619	7525M	Hunter F.1	Sectioned
WZ736	7868M	Avro 707A	–
XG454	8366M	Belvedere HC.1	–
XL824	8021M	Sycamore HR.14	–
100549		Fa 330A-1	Loan
J-1172	8487M	Vampire FB.6	–

M A N C H E S T E R   A I R P O R T
(Or Ringway)

G-ARPK	Trident 1C	Fire
G-BAWV	Aztec 250B	Fire
G-BCCJ	AA-5 Traveler	Stored

M O S T O N
(On the B6393 north of Manchester)

G-ATOO	Cherokee 140	Inst, North Manchester College
G-AXYX	Ekin Airbuggy	Spares

R O Y T O N
(On the A627 north of Oldham)   1855
Squadron ATC, Park Lane

WS726	7960M	Meteor NF.14	Gate
XK637		Vampire T.11	Inst

S T O C K P O R T

G-AXUY	SAN DR.100A	Stored

T I M P E R L E Y
(On the A560 east of Altrincham)   145
Squadron, ATC

WD318	8207M	Chipmunk T.10	PAX tnr

W I G A N
The Aeroplane Collection store.

G-AFIU	LA.4 Minor	–
BAPC 17	Woodhams Sprite	Frame
BAPC 60	Murray Helicopter	–

W O O D F O R D
British   Aerospace   Avro   Aircraft
Restoration Society   General enquiries
about   the   Society   can   be   made   to :
Harry   Holmes,   British   Aerospace   plc,
Woodford, Cheshire SK7 1QR.

G-AHKX	Avro XIX Srs 2	Restn
XM603	Vulcan B.2A	Stored

British Aerospace

c/n 1808	HS.748-2B	Stored
c/n 1809	HS.748-2B	Stored
XV148	Nimrod prot	Fatigue rig
XV257	Nimrod MR.2	Stored
c/n 06402	Comet 4	Fuselage
	Andover	Test shell

Merseyside

BIRKDALE
(On the A565 south west of Southport)
281 Squadron ATC, Upper Aughton Road

WG477	8362M	Chipmunk T.10	PAX tnr

LIVERPOOL AIRPORT
(Or Speke)

G-AVWF	Cherokee 140	Stored
G-BIZL	Nord 3202	Stored
G-OCME	Trislander	Spares

MEOLS

WZ514	Vampire T.11	-

WOODVALE

WA591	7917M	Meteor T.7	Gate
WG418	8209M	Chipmunk T.10	PAX tnr

West Midlands

ALLESLEY
(On the A4114 north west of Coventry)

G-AFHA	Mosscraft MA.1	Stored
G-AFJV	Mosscraft MA.2	Stored
G-AKUW	Super Ace 2	Restn

BERKSWELL
(Between the A452 and the A45 west of Coventry)

G-AFJA		Watkinson Dingbat	Stored
DR613	G-AFJB	GM.1 Wicko	Restn

BIRMINGHAM
Museum of Science and Industry   Open Monday to Saturday 0930 to 1700 and Sunday 1400 to 1700. Contact : Birmingham Museum of Science and Industry, Newhall Street, Birmingham B3 1RZ. Telephone 021 236 1022.

KX829		Hurricane IV	-
ML427	6457M	Spitfire IX	-
		Beaufighter I	Nose

Haslucks Green Barracks

WT534	8549M	Canberra PR.7	Nose, ATC
XS886	A2685	Wessex HAS.1	Inst, Navy
		Jet Provost	Nose, ATC

2030 Squadron ATC, Barrows Lane, Sheldon

WD646	8189M	Meteor TT.20	-

2371 Squadron ATC, Gressel Lane, Tile Cross

WZ450	Vampire T.11	Pod

Others, Shirley

G-ASLF	Bensen B-7	Stored
	Bensen	Stored

BIRMINGHAM AIRPORT
(Or Elmdon)

G-AWZZ	Trident 3B-101	Fire
BAPC 9	Humber Mono	Terminal

COVENTRY
163 Squadron ATC, Smith Street

	Valiant	Nose
	Jet Provost T.3	Nose

Others, locally

G-AFSV	Chilton DW.1A	Restn
G-BMSB	MJ627	Spitfire Tr IX	Restn
BAPC 27	Mignet HM.14	Stored

SOLIHULL

G-ASRE	Aztec 250C	Trials

STONNALL
(On the A452 south east of Brownhills)

G-AYOL	Horizon 180	Stored

SUTTON COLDFIELD
St George's Barracks, Rectory Road

XR777"	XT625	Scout AH.1	Gate

Locally

G-AEUJ	Whitney Straight	Restn
G-AFRZ	Monarch	Stored

Norfolk

COLTISHALL

		Hurricane replica	Gate
WE173	8740M	Canberra PR.3	Fire
WT745	8893M	Hunter T.8C	Inst
XG254	8881M	Hunter FGA.9	BDRT
XM172	8427M	Lightning F.1A	For tender
XV747		Harrier GR.3	BDRT
XX109	8918M	Jaguar GR.1	WLT
XX734	8816M	Jaguar GR.1	Fuselage

FAKENHAM

G-ASCH	Terrier 2	Restn

FELTHORPE

G-ARBG	Nipper II	Restn

GREAT YARMOUTH AIRFIELD

(Or North Denes)

G-BKGD	WG.30-100	Stored
G-KATE	WG.30-100	Stored
G-OGAS	WG.30-100	Stored

KING'S LYNN

Locally

XS420	Lightning T.5	Stored
XS459	Lightning T.5	Stored
XS933	Lightning F.6	Nose

LUDHAM

G-FIST		Fi 156C-3 Storch	Restn
TE566	G-BLCK	Spitfire IX	Restn

MARHAM

WH863	8693M	Canberra T.17	BDRT
XA917	7827M	Victor B.1	Nose
XH560		Vulcan K.2	Fire
XH673	8911M	Victor K.2	Gate
XL160	8910M	Victor K.2	Spares
XX947	8797M	Tornado P.03	WLT
XL192		Victor K.2	Fire

NEATISHEAD

(In between the A149, A1062 and A151 north east of Norwich)

WK654	8092M	Meteor F.8	Gate

NORWICH AIRPORT

(Or Horsham St Faith) City of Norwich Aviation Museum   The Museum is open on Sundays October to April 1000 to 1300 and May to September 1000 to 1700 and on Thursday evenings during June, July and August from 1930 to dusk. Contact : City of Norwich Aviation Museum, Old Norwich Road, Horsham St Faiths, Norwich, Norfolk.

G-ASKK		Herald 211	-
TX228		Anson C.19	-
XD375	7887M	Vampire T.11	-
XL840		Whirlwind HAS.7	-
XM612		Vulcan B.2A	-
XP355	G-BEBC	Whirlwind HAR.10	-
XP458		Grasshopper TX.1	Loan
XP919	8163M	Sea Vixen FAW.2	-
121		Mystere IVA	-
16718		T-33A-5-LO	-

Airport

G-AVEZ	Herald 210	Fire
G-AVPN	Herald 213	Stored

OLD BUCKENHAM

(On the B1077 south of Attleborough)

G-AODT		Tiger Moth	Restn
G-APOI		Skeeter 8	Stored
G-BENL		Pawnee 235D	Spares
XL812	G-SARO	Skeeter AOP.12	Restn

RAVENINGHAM

(On the B1136 north of Beccles)

G-AYDR	SNCAN SV-4C	Restn
G-BEPF	SNCAN SV-4A	Restn
N30228	J-3C-65 Cub	Restn

REYMERSTON HALL

G-ATHL		Wallis WA-116/F	Spares
G-AZBU	XR246	Auster AOP.9	Stored
G-AZVA		Monsun 150FF	Stored
G-BGKT	XN441	Auster AOP.9	Stored

SCULTHORPE

42212	F-100D-11-NA	Gate

SHIPDHAM

G-AYAF		Twin Comanche	Stored
G-BINH		Tiger Moth	Restn
VT-CZV	G-AISY	Tiger Moth	Stored
VT-DOU	HU483	Tiger Moth	Stored
VT-DOX	HU492	Tiger Moth	Stored
VT-DOY	HU498	Tiger Moth	Stored
VT-DOZ	HU504	Tiger Moth	Stored
VT-DPA	HU511	Tiger Moth	Stored
VT-DPB	HU708	Tiger Moth	Stored
VT-DPC	HU187"	Tiger Moth	Stored
VT-DPE	HU858	Tiger Moth	Stored
VT-DPH	HU887	Tiger Moth	Stored
N9191	G-ALND	Tiger Moth	Restn

SWANTON MORLEY

G-BFIP	Wallbro Monoplane	Stored
WB626	Chipmunk T.10	Spares
WJ775	8581M Canberra B.6RC	Inst
XV152	8776M Buccaneer S.2A	Inst

THORPE ABBOTTS
(On the A143 east of Diss) 100th Bomb
Group Tower Museum

CF-EPV	Carvair	Cockpit

WATTON

WS807	7973M Meteor NF.14	Gate

WEST RAYNHAM

XH980	7867M Javelin FAW.8	Gate

Northamptonshire

EAST HADDON
(North of the A428 north west of
Northampton)

G-AVIP	Brantly B.2B	Stored

**HINTON-IN-THE-
HEDGES**

G-AWCJ	Cessna F.150H	Wreck

KINGS CLIFFE
(South of the A47, west of
Peterborough)

G-BEUS	AIA SV-4C	Restn

NORTHAMPTON

G-AFPR	Moth Minor	Restn

NORTHAMPTON AIRPORT
(Or Sywell)

G-AIZZ	J/1 Autocrat	Restn
G-AWRA	Pup 100	Fuselage
G-AYIA	Hughes 369HS	Spares
G-BKJR	Hughes 269C	Pod
G-BOXS	Hughes 269C	Wreck
G-HEWS	Hughes 369D	Wreck

WELLINGBOROUGH
Locally

G-APKY	Hiller UH-12B	Stored
G-BGTB	TB-10 Tobago	Fuselage
MD497" G-ANLW	Widgeon	Stored
WP784	Chipmunk T.10	PAX tnr

Northumberland

BOULMER

XP745	8453M Lightning F.3	Gate

CURROCK HILL

WK549	Chipmunk T.10	Stored

OTTERBURN RANGES
(On the A696 north of Newcastle-on-
Tyne)

XF386	8707M Hunter F.6A	-

XG264	8715M Hunter FGA.9	Composite
XJ604	8222M Sea Vixen FAW.2	-
XP515	8614M Gnat T.1	-
XP694	Lightning F.3	-
XP702	Lightning F.3	-
XS594	Andover C.1	Fuselage
XS601	Andover C.1	-

Nottinghamshire

BALDERTON
(On the A1 south east of Newark-on-Trent)
XN728   8546M Lightning F.2A Displayed

FIRBECK
(West of the A60 north of Worksop)
South Yorkshire Aircraft Preservation Society   Visits are possible at weekends, further details from : SYAS, Home Farm, Firbeck, near Worksop, Nottinghamshire. Tel 0709 812168

Reg		Type	Note
G-AEKR"	B'121	Mignet HM.14	–
G-ALYB	RT520	Auster 5	Restn
G-AWFH		Cessna F.150H	Fuselage
A4850"	B'176	SE.5A scale rep	–
XD435		Vampire T.11	–
XE864		Vampire T.11	–
XE935		Vampire T.11	Composite
XM279		Canberra B(I).8	Nose
		Vampire FB.5	Pod, loan
E-424	G-9-445	Hunter F.51	Fuselage

LANGAR
Reg	Type	Note
G-BATD	Cessna U.206F	Para-tnr

MANSFIELD
384 Squadron ATC
Reg		Type	Note
WT507	8548M	Canberra PR.7	Nose

NEWARK-ON-TRENT
Reg		Type	Note
G-AIGR		J/1N Alpha	Stored
G-AIJI		J/1N Alpha	Stored
G-AIKE		Auster 5	Restn
G-AKOT		Auster 5	Spares
G-AKWT		Auster 5	Frame
G-ALNV		Auster 5	Frame
G-AMUJ		J/5F Aiglet Tnr	Wreck
G-ANHW		Auster 5D	Stored
G-ANHX		Auster 5D	Restn
G-AOCP		Auster 5	Restn
G-ARGB		Auster 6A	Stored
G-ARGI		Auster 6A	Frame
G-AROJ		Airedale	Stored
G-ARTM		Terrier 1	Wreck
G-ASWF		Airedale	Stored
EC-AXR	G-ANHU	Auster 4	Restn
F-BBSO	G-AMJM	Auster 5	Frame
	c/n 3705	Auster D.6/180	Frame
	c/n 608	Terrier 2	Frame

NEWTON
Reg		Type	Note
WT694	7510M	Hunter F.1	Gate
XL623	8770M	Hunter T.7	Inst
XN641	8865M	Jet Provost T.3	Fire

NOTTINGHAM AIRPORT
(Or Tollerton)
Reg	Type	Note
G-AGVJ	J/1N Alpha	Stored

SOUTH SCARLE
(In between the A46 and the A1133 south west of Lincoln)
Reg	Type	Note
G-AZEE	MS.880B Rallye	Stored

STAPLEFORD
(On the A453 south west of Nottingham)
1360 Squadron ATC, Cliff Hill Avenue
Reg		Type	Note
XD463	8023M	Vampire T.11	–

SYERSTON
Reg		Type	Note
WZ791	8944M	Grasshopper TX.1	Stored
XE799	8943M	Cadet TX.3	Stored
XN185	8942M	Sedbergh TX.1	Stored

WINTHORPE
(On the A46 north east of Newark-on-Trent) Newark air Museum   The Museum is open April to October Monday to Friday 1000 to 1700, Saturday 1300 to 1700 and Sundays 1000 to 1800. November to March, Sundays only 1000 to dusk. All buildings are available to the disabled, as are the toilets. Contact : Mick Smith, Curator, Newark Air Museum, 35 Queen Street, Balderton, Newark, Notts, NG24 3NS. Museum telephone : 0636 707170.

Reg		Type	Note
G-AHRI		Dove 1B	–
G-AHMP		Proctor II	Cockpit
G-ANXB		Heron 1	Restn
BAPC 20		Lee Richards rep	Stored
BAPC183		Zurowski ZP.1	
VH-UTH		Monospar ST-12	Stored
KF532		Harvard IIB	Cockpit
TG517		Hastings T.5	–
VL348	G-AVVO	Anson C.19	–
VR249	G-APIY	Prentice T.1	–
VT229	7151M	Meteor F.4	–
VZ608		Meteor FR.9(mod)	–
VZ634	8657M	Meteor T.7	–
WF369		Varsity T.1	–
WH904		Canberra T.19	–
WK277	7719M	Swift FR.5	–
WM913	8162M	Sea Hawk FB.3	–
WR977	8186M	Shackleton MR.3/3	–
WS692	7605M	Meteor NF.12	–
WS739	7961M	Meteor NF.14	–
WT933	7709M	Sycamore 3	–
WV606	7622M	Provost T.1	–
WV787	8799M	Canberra B.2/8	–
WW217		Sea Venom FAW.21	–
WX905	7458M	Venom NF.3	–

WZ553		Vampire T.11	Stored
XD515	7998M	Vampire T.11	-
XD593		Vampire T.11	Stored
XE317		Sycamore HR.14	-
XH992	7829M	Javelin FAW.8	-
XJ560	8142M	Sea Vixen FAW.2	-
XL149	7988M	Beverley C.1	Nose
XL764	7940M	Skeeter AOP.12	-
XM594		Vulcan B.2A	-
XM685		Whirlwind HAS.7	-

XN511		Jet Provost T.3	Nose
XN819	8205M	Argosy C.1	Cockpit
XN964		Buccaneer S.1	-
XP226	A2667	Gannet AEW.3	-
XS417		Lightning T.5	-
XT200		Sioux AH.1	-
51-9036		T-33A-1-LO	-
54-2223		F-100D-16-NA	-
83		Mystere IVA	-
56321	G-BKPY	Safir	-

Oxfordshire

A B I N G D O N

RAFEF = Royal Air Force Exhibition Flight, travelling recruiting airframes.

TB382	7244M	Spitfire XVI	RAFEF
TE311	7241M	Spitfire XVI	RAFEF
WH703	8490M	Canberra B.2	BDRT
WH869	8515M	Canberra B.2	Inst
WJ678	8864M	Canberra B.2	BDRT
WJ876		Canberra T.4	Nose, RAFEF
WK146		Canberra B.2	Nose, RAFEF
XE643	8586M	Hunter FGA.9	Nose, RAFEF
XE670	8585M	Hunter F.4	Nose, RAFEF
XG226	8800M	Hunter F.6A	Fuselage
XH537	8749M	Vulcan B.2MRR	Stored
XK943	8796M	Whirlwind HAS.7	Dump
XL569	8833M	Hunter T.7	BDRT
XM191	8590M	Lightning F.1	Nose, RAFEF
XN137		Jet Provost T.3	Nose, RAFEF
XN503		Jet Provost T.3	Nose, RAFEF
XN962	8183M	Buccaneer S.1	Nose, RAFEF
XP541	8616M	Gnat T.1	BDRT
XT274	8856M	Buccaneer S.2A	BDRT
XT284	8855M	Buccaneer S.2A	BDRT
XT595	8851M	Phantom FG.1	Nose, RAFEF
XV259		Nimrod AEW.3	Stored
XV261		Nimrod AEW.3	Dump
XV262		Nimrod AEW.3	Dump
XV337	8852M	Buccaneer S.2C	BDRT
XV338	8774M	Buccaneer S.2A	Nose, RAFEF
XV753		Harrier Gr.3	BDRT
XV784	8909M	Harrier Gr.3	BDRT
XX115	8821M	Jaguar GR.1	Dump
XX162"	B'152	Hawk T.1 replica	RAFEF
XX262"	B'171	Hawk T.1 replica	RAFEF
XX344	8847M	Hawk T.1	BDRT
XX396	8718M	Gazelle HT.3	RAFEF
XX718"	B'150	Jaguar GR.1 rep	RAFEF
XX824"	B'151	Jaguar GR.1 rep	RAFEF
XZ135	8848M	Harrier GR.3	Nose, RAFEF
XZ280		Nimrod AEW.3	Stored
XZ281		Nimrod AEW.3	Stored
XZ282		Nimrod AEW.3	Stored
XZ283		Nimrod AEW.3	Stored
XZ285		Nimrod AEW.3	Stored
XZ286		Nimrod AEW.3	Dump
XZ287		Nimrod AEW.3	Stored
ZA322"	B'155	Tornado GR.1 rep	RAFEF
ZD230	G-ASGA	Super VC-10 1151	Stored
ZD235	G-ASGG	Super VC-10 1151	Stored
ZD240	G-ASGL	Super VC-10 1151	Stored
ZD241	G-ASGM	Super VC-10 1151	Stored
ZD242	G-ASGP	Super VC-10 1151	Stored
ZD243	G-ASGR	Super VC-10 1151	Stored
ZD472"	B'191	Harrier GR.5 rep	RAFEF
	G-ALYW	'Nimrod MR.1'	Fuselage

A R N C O T T

(South of the A41 south east of Bicester)

G-ASEF		Auster 6A	Restn

B E N S O N

G-ARRV	8669M	HS.748MF	Fire dump
		Spitfire replica	Gate
XR509	8752M	Wessex HC.2	BDRT
XS642	8785M	Andover C.1	Inst
10639	8478M	Bf 109G-2	Restn

B I C E S T E R

G-ASRI		Aztec 250B	Spares
WB556		Chipmunk T.10	Spares
WB645	8218M	Chipmunk T.10	Fuselage
WG300		Chipmunk T.10	Spares
WG303	8208M"	Chipmunk T.10	Test-bed

B R I Z E   N O R T O N

6V-AEE	Cessna A.150M	Sapres
WT684	7422M Hunter F.1	Dump
XS479	8819M Wessex HU.5	Inst
XS598	Andover C.1	Fuselage
XT141	8509M Sioux AH.1	Inst
XT486	8919M Wessex HU.5	Inst
XT677	8016M Wessex HC.2	Dump
XV638	8826M Wasp HAS.1	Inst
XX914	8777M VC-10 1103	Fuselage
ZD234	8700M Super VC-10 1151	Nose
ZD493	G-ARVJ VC-10 1101	Stored

C H A L G R O V E

WA638	Meteor T.7	Spares

C U L H A M
(On the A415 south east of Abingdon)
Lightning Studies Unit

WV381	Hunter GA.11	Fuselage

E N S T O N E

G-BEIH	Pawnee 235D	Restn
	Pawnee	Frame

H E N L E Y - O N - T H A M E S
Berkshire Aviation Group, store. For
further details contact : 45 Malvern
Way, Twyford, Berkshire RG10 9PY.

G-AHUI	Messenger 2A	Fuselage
G-AJFF	Messenger 2A	Stored
G-AKER	Gemini 1A	Cockpit
G-AKGD	Gemini 1A	Sectioned
G-AKHZ	Gemini 7	Composite

O X F O R D   A I R P O R T
(Or Kidlington)

G-ARJR		Apache 160G	Inst
G-ARMA		Apache 160G	Inst
G-ASEW		Brantly B.2B	Inst
G-AVBU		Cherokee Six 260	Inst
G-BBVI		Enstrom F-28A	Inst
G-BDBZ	XJ398	Whirlwind HAR.10	Inst
G-BFSK		Apache 160	Inst
G-SHOE		Cessna 421C II	Fuselage
XT175	TAD175	Sioux AH.1	Inst

S H O T T E S W E L L
(Off the A41 north of Banbury)

G-BCLS	Cessna 170B	Stored

S H R I V E N H A M
(On the A420 north east of Swindon)
Royal Military College of Science

WZ706	7851M Auster AOP.9	Inst
XT151	Sioux AH.1	Stored
XT621	Scout AH.1	Inst

U P P E R   H E Y F O R D

36	EABDR8	Mystere IVA	BDRT
46	EABDR9	Mystere IVA	BDRT
127	EABDR7	Mystere IVA	BDRT
129	EABDR6	Mystere IVA	BDRT
62-4428		F-105G-RE	BDRT
63-7449		F-4C-17-MC	BDRT

Shropshire

B R I D G N O R T H

XH330	Vampire T.11	Composite

C H E T W Y N D

G-ATIE	Cessna 150F	Para-tnr

C O S F O R D
Aerospace Museum and British Airways
Annex Open daily, April to October
1000 to 1600 and weekdays only 1000 to
1600 November to March. Contact :
Aerospace Museum, RAF Cosford,
Shifnal, Shropshire, TF11 8UP.
Telephone 090 722 4872 or '4112.

G-AFAP	"T2B-272 CASA 352L		-
G-AGRU		Viking 1	-
G-AJOV"	WP495 Dragonfly HR.3		-
G-AMOG		Viscount 701	-
G-AOVF		Britannia 312F	-
G-APAS	8351M Comet 1XB		-
G-APFJ		Boeing 707-436	-
G-ARPH		Trident 1C	-
G-ARVM		VC-10 1101	-
BAPC 94	8583M Fi 103 (V1)		-
BAPC 99	8486M Ohka II		-
K7271"	B'148 Fury I replica		-
DG202/G	5758M F.9/40 Meteor		-
KG374"	KN645 Dakota IV		-
KN751		B-24L-20-FO Liberator	-
MT847	6960M Spitfire XIV		-
RF398	8376M Lincoln B.2		-
TA639	7806M Mosquito TT.35		-
TG511	8554M Hastings T.5		-
TS798	G-AGNV York C.1		-
TX214	7817M Anson C.19		-
VP952	8820M Devon C.2/2		-
VV106	7175M Supermarine 517		-
VX272	7174M Hawker P.1052		-

VX573	8389M	Valetta C.3	-
WA634		Meteor T.7(mod)	-
WB188	7154M	Hawker P.1067	-
WF408	8395M	Varsity T.1	-
WG760	7755M	EE P.1A	-
WG768	8005M	Short SB.5	-
WG777	7986M	Fairey FD-2	-
WK935	7869M	Meteor F.8(mod)	-
WL732		Sea Balliol T.21	-
WP912	8467M	Chipmunk T.10	-
WT346	8197M	Canberra B(I).8	-
WT555	7499M	Hunter F.1	-
WV562	7606M	Provost T.1	-
WV746	8938M	Pembroke C.1	-
WZ744	7932M	Avro 707	-
XA564	7464M	Javelin FAW.1	-
XA893	8591M	Vulcan B.1	Nose
XD145		SARO SR.53	-
XD674	7570M	Jet Provost T.1	-
XF926	8368M	Bristol T.188	-
XG337	8056M	Lightning F.1	-
XH592	8429M	Victor K.1A	-
XJ389	G-AJJP	Jet Gyrodyne	-
XJ918	8190M	Sycamore HR.14	-
XK724	7715M	Gnat F.1	-
XL703	8034M	Pioneer CC.1	-
XL993	8388M	Twin Pioneer CC.1	-
XM555	8027M	Skeeter AOP.12	-
XM598	8778M	Vulcan B.2A	-
XN714		Hunting 126	-
XP299	8726M	Whirlwind HAR.10	-
XP411	8442M	Argosy C.1	-
XR220	7933M	TSR-2 XO-2	-
XR371		Belfast C.1	-
XR977	8640M	Gnat T.1	-
XS770		Basset CC.1	-
ZD485	A-515	FMA Pucara	-
204		SP-2H Neptune	-
J-1704		Venom FB.4	-
L-866	8466M	PBY-6A Catalina	-
191614	8481M	Me 163B-1a	-
	8469M	Fa 330A-1	-
17473		T-33A-1-LO	-

2 School of Technical Training and
Weapons School (latter marked *)

WH740	8762M	Canberra T.17	-
WH775	8868M	Canberra PR.7	-
WH957	8869M	Canberra PR.7	-
WH960	8344M	Canberra B.15	-
WH964	8870M	Canberra E.15	-
WH984	8101M	Canberra B.15	-
WJ565	8871M	Canberra T.17	-
WJ640	8722M	Canberra B.2	-
WJ756		Canberra E.15	-
WK102	8780M	Canberra T.17	-
WT532	8890M	Canberra PR.7	-
WT536	8063M	Canberra PR.7	-
XG225	8713M	Hunter F.6A	Displayed
XH136	8782M	Canberra PR.9	-
XH171	8746M	Canberra PR.9	-

XH593	8428M	Victor K.1A	-
XM351	8078M	Jet Provost T.3	-
XM367	8083M	Jet Provost T.3	-
XM455		Jet Provost T.3A	-
XM471		Jet Provost T.3A	-
XN472		Jet Provost T.3A	-
XN492	8079M	Jet Provost T.3	-
XN501		Jet Provost T.3A	-
XN582		Jet Provost T.3A	-
XN594	8077M	Jet Provost T.3	-
XP338	8647M	Whirlwind HAR.10	-
XP533	8632M	Gnat T.1	-
XP538	8607M	Gnat T.1	-
XP547		Jet Provost T.4	-
XR537	8642M	Gnat T.1	-
XR679		Jet Provost T.4	-
XS102	8624M	Gnat T.1	-
XS105	8625M	Gnat T.1	-
XS107	8639M	Gnat T.1	-
XS178		Jet Provost T.4	-
XS219		Jet Provost T.4	-
XT277	8853M	Buccaneer S.2A	-
XT466	8921M	Wessex HU.5	-
XW544	8857M	Buccaneer S.2C	-
XX110	8955M	Jaguar GR.1	-
XX727	8951M	Jaguar GR.1	-
XX730	8952M	Jaguar GR.1	-
XX751	8937M	Jaguar GR.1	-
XX756	8899M	Jaguar GR.1	-
XX819	8923M	Jaguar GR.1	-
XX948	8879M	Tornado P.06	*
XX959	8953M	Jaguar GR.1	-
XX969	8897M	Jaguar GR.1	-
XZ368	8900M	Jaguar GR.1	-
XZ371	8907M	Jaguar GR.1	*
XZ383	8901M	Jaguar GR.1	-
XZ384	8954M	Jaguar GR.1	-
		Lightning F.2A	Nose*
		Lightning F.3	Nose*
		Buccaneer S.2	Nose*

L U D L O W

G-ABUS	Comper Swift	Stored
G-AHLT	Tiger Moth	Stored
G-BADV	MB.50 Pipistrelle	Stored

O S W E S T R Y

G-AYOV	Cessna FA.150L	Cockpit

S H A W B U R Y

LA226	7119M	Spitfire F.21	Stored
WH724		Canberra T.19	Nose
WK511		Chipmunk T.10	Stored
WT799		Hunter T.8	Stored
XD382	8033M	Vampire T.11	Gate
XM927	8814M	Wessex HAS.3	Dump
XN977		Buccaneer S.2B	Stored
XP351	8672M	Whirlwind HAR.10	Gate
XP771		Beaver AL.1	Stored

XP775	Beaver AL.1	Stored		XX826	Jaguar GR.1	Stored
XP779	Beaver AL.1	Stored		XX841	Jaguar T.2	Stored
XP810	Beaver AL.1	Stored		XX847	Jaguar T.2	Stored
XP814	Beaver AL.1	Stored		XX887	Buccaneer S.2B	Stored
XT270	Buccaneer S.2B	Stored		XX888	Buccaneer S.2B	Stored
XT275	Buccaneer S.2B	Stored		XX896	Buccaneer S.2B	Stored
XT276	Buccaneer S.2B	Stored		XX958	Jaguar GR.1	Stored
XV157	Buccaneer S.2B	Stored		XX967	Jaguar GR.1	Stored
XV268	Beaver AL.1	Stored		XX968	Jaguar GR.1	Stored
XV334	Buccaneer S.2B	Stored		XX977	Jaguar GR.1	Stored
XV336	Buccaneer S.2B	Stored		XZ370	Jaguar GR.1	Stored
XV349	Buccaneer S.2B	Stored		XZ374	Jaguar GR.1	Stored
XV356	Buccaneer S.2B	Stored		XZ381	Jaguar GR.1	Stored
XV866	Buccaneer S.2B	Stored		XZ390	Jaguar GR.1	Stored
XX121	Jaguar GR.1	Stored				
XX140	Jaguar T.2	Stored		**T E R N H I L L**		
XX722	Jaguar GR.1	Stored		XH274	Vampire T.11	Dump
XX744	Jaguar GR.1	Stored				
XX753	Jaguar GR.1	Stored		**T I L S T O C K**		
XX763	Jaguar GR.1	Stored		G-ASNN	Cessna 182F	Para-tnr
XX764	Jaguar GR.1	Stored				
XX824	Jaguar GR.1	Stored		**W H I T C H U R C H**		
XX825	Jaguar GR.1	Stored		XD452	7990M Vampire T.11	-

Somerset

C H I L T O N   C A N T E L O
(Just south of Yeovilton)
WM983   Sea Hawk FGA.6 Composite

G L A S T O N B U R Y
XP399   Whirlwind HAR.10   -

H E N S T R I D G E
G-AHSD	T'craft Plus D	Stored
G-AISC	Tipsy B Srs 1	Restn
G-ALYG	Auster 5D	Stored
G-ANEW	Tiger Moth	Stored
G-ARJD	Colt 108	Stored

W E L L S
1955 Squadron ATC, Webbs Close
WD355" WD335 Chipmunk T.10   PAX tnr

Y E O V I L
Locally
G-AOXN   Tiger Moth   Restn

Y E O V I L T O N
Fleet Air Museum and Concorde Exhibition Open every day (other than Christmas) March to October 1000 to 1730 and November to February 1000 to 1630. Contact : Fleet Air Arm Museum, RNAS Yeovilton, Ilchester, Somerset, BA22 8HT. Telephone : 0935 840 565.

G-AZAZ		Bensen B-8	-
G-BSST		Concorde 002	-
BAPC 58		Ohka II	Loan
BAPC149		Short S.27 replica	-
8359		Short 184	Nose, loan
B6401"	G-AWYY	Camel replica	-
L2301	G-AIZG	Walrus I	-
L2940		Skua I	Remains
N1854	G-AIBE	Fulmar II	-
N2078"		Sopwith Baby	Composite
N4389"	N4172	Albacore	-
N5226"	N5903	Gladiator II	-
N5492"	B'111	Sopwith Triplane rep	-
N6452	G-BIAU	Pup replica	-
P4139"	HS618	Swordfish II	-
AL246		Martlet I	-
DP872		Barracuda	Remains
EX976		Harvard IIA	-
KD431		Corsair IV	-
KE209		Hellcat II	-
LZ551/G		Sea Vampire I	Loan
SX137		Seafire F.17	-
VR137		Wyvern TF.1	-
WA473		Attacker F.1	-
WG774		BAC 221	-
WJ231		Sea Fury FB.11	-
WN493		Dragonfly HR.5	-
WT121		Skyraider AEW.1	-
WV856		Sea Hawk FGA.6	-
WW138		Sea Venom FAW.22	-

XA127		Sea Vampire T.22	Nose
XB446		Avenger AS.4	-
XB480	A2577	Hiller HT.1	-
XD317		Scimitar F.1	-
XG574	A2575	Whirlwind HAR.3	-
XJ314		Rolls-Royce TMR	-
XJ402	A2572	Whirlwind HAS.3	-
XK488		Buccaneer S.1	-
XL503		Gannet AEW.3	-
XL717	G-AOXG	Tiger Moth	-
XN957		Buccaneer S.1	-
XP142		Wessex HAS.3	-
XP841		HP.115	-
XS527		Wasp HAS.1	-
XS590		Sea Vixen FAW.2	-
XT176		Sioux AH.1	-
XT596		Phantom FG.1	-
		Gannet AS	Cockpit
A-522	8768M	FMA Pucara	-
0729		T-34C-1 Turbo Mentor	-
0767		MB.339AA	-
S3398	G-BFYO	SPAD XIII replica	-
D5397"	G-BFXL	Albatros D.Va replica	-
102/17"	B'88	Fokker Dr I scale rep	-

155848		F-4S-MC Phantom II	-
159233		AV-8A-MC Harrier	-
01420	G-BMZF	MiG 15bis (LIM-2)	-

Fleet Air Arm Historic Aircraft Flight

T8191		Tiger Moth	-
LS326	G-AJVH	Swordfish II	-
TF956		Sea Fury FB.11	-
WB271		Firefly AS.5	-
WG655		Sea Fury T.20S	-
WV908	A2660	Sea Hawk FGA.6	-

Others

WJ677		Canberra B.2	Nose
WP309		Sea Prince T.1	Fire
XE369	A2633	Sea Hawk FGA.6	Fire
XM845	A2682	Wessex HAS.1	Fire
XN308	A2605	Whirlwind HAS.7	Fire
XN692	A2624	Sea Vixen FAW.2	Gate
XS128	A2670	Wessex HAS.1	BDRT
XV277		Harrier GR.3	Inst

Staffordshire

ALDRIDGE
425 Squadron ATC, Station Road

WD931	Canberra B.2	Nose

BURNTWOOD

XM652	Vulcan B.2A	Nose

HALFPENNY GREEN

BGA.1346	T.31	Air Scouts

LICHFIELD
1206 Squadron ATC, Cherry Orchard Rd

WK576	8357M	Chipmunk T.10	PAX tnr

Scrapyard

XL471	Gannet AEW.3	-

PENKRIDGE
(On the A449 south of Stafford) 2415
Squadron ATC, Grange Lane

XD528	8159M	Vampire T.11	-

ROCESTER
(On the B5030 north of Uttoxeter)

G-ARJB	Dove 8	Stored

STAFFORD

XA801	7739M	Javelin FAW.2	Gate
XP359	8447M	Whirlwind HAR.10	BDR
XS572	8845M	Wasp HAS.1	Dump
XT469	8920M	Wessex HU.5	BDR

STOKE-ON-TRENT
City Museum and Art Gallery   Open
daily 1030 to 1700 Monday to Saturday
and Sundays 1400 to 1700. Contact :
Stoke-on-Trent City Museum and Art
Gallery, Bethesda Street, Hanley,
Stoke ST1 3DE. Tel 0782 273173.

RW388	6946M	Spitfire XVI	-

Ken Fern Collection   Visits by prior
permission only : 311 Congleton Road,
Scholar Green, Stoke-on-Trent, ST7 3JQ

G-AFIN		Chrislea Airguard	Restn
RA854		Cadet TX.1	-

SWYNNERTON
(East of the A519 south of Newcastle-
under-Lyne)

XK987	8393M	Whirlwind HAR.10	Inst

TATENHILL

G-ARNN	GC-1B Swift	Restn
G-AVLM	Pup 160	Restn
G-BFNM	GC-1B Swift	Restn

Suffolk

BAWDSEY
(At the end of the B1083, south east of Woodbridge)
XE673   8846M Hunter GA.11   BDR

BENTWATERS
80260   F-101B-105-MC Voodoo BDR
104   Mystere IVA   BDR

BURY ST EDMUNDS
VV217   7323M Vampire FB.5   -
WG471   8210M Chipmunk T.10   PAX tnr
WK575   Chipmunk T.10   Wreck

FLIXTON
(On the B1062 west of Bungay) Norfolk and Suffolk Aviation Museum Open: April, May, September and October open Sundays and Bank Holidays 1000-1700; July and August open Wednesdays and Thursdays 1900-2100; June, July and August on Sundays 1000-2100; July and August on Thursdays 1100-1700. Contact : The Secretary, Norfolk and Suffolk Aviation Museum, Flixton, Bungay, Suffolk.
BAPC 147   Bensen B.7   -
N99153   T-28C Trojan   Fuselage
P9390" BAPC71 Spitfire replica   -
VL349   G-AWSA Anson C.19   -
VX580   Valetta C.2   Loan
WF128   8611M Sea Prince T.1   -
WF643   Meteor F.8   Composite
WV605   Provost T.1   -
XH892   7982M Javelin FAW.9R   Loan
XJ482   A2598 Sea Vixen FAW.1   -
XK624   Vampire T.11   -
XN304   Whirlwind HAS.7   -
XR485   Whirlwind HAR.10   -
42196   F-100D-11-NA S'Sabre -
54433   T-33A-5-LO   -
79   Mystere IVA   -

HONINGTON
XK526   8648M Buccaneer S.1   Gate
XN930   8180M Buccaneer S.1   Dump
XR754   Lightning F.6   Dump
XV338   8774M Buccaneer S.2A   Cockpit
XX886   Buccaneer S.2B   WLT
XX946   8883M Tornado P.02   WLT
ZA408   Tornado GR.1   Wreck
ZA494   Tornado GR.1   Wreck
ZA555   Tornado GR.1   Wreck

IPSWICH
188 Squadron ATC, TAVR Centre
WG463   8363M Chipmunk T.10   PAX tnr

IPSWICH AIRPORT
G-ARKM   Colt 108   Restn
G-ATES   Cherokee Six   Para-tnr
G-BJWL   BN-2 Islander   Stored
G-BJWM   BN-2 Islander   Stored
G-BJWN   BN-2 Islander   Stored
N750M   Grumman Widgeon   Spares
N3103Q G-DUCK Grumman Widgeon   Restn
N4565L   DC-3-201A   Stored

LAKENHEATH
24434   F-105G-RE Voodoo   BDRT
37471   F-4C-18-MC Phantom   BDRT
37610   F-4C-20-MC Phantom   BDRT
63319" 42269 F-100D-16-NA   Gate
16   Mystere IVA   Decoy
75   Mystere IVA   Decoy
99   Mystere IVA   Decoy
113   Mystere IVA   Decoy
126   Mystere IVA   Decoy
145   Mystere IVA   Decoy
241   Mystere IVA   Decoy
285   Mystere IVA   Decoy
300   Mystere IVA   Decoy
309   Mystere IVA   Decoy

MILDENHALL
16769   T-33A-1-LO   BDRT
24198   VC-140B-LM JetStar   Inst
40707   F-4C-22-MC Phantom   BDRT

MONEWDEN
(South of the A1120, north of Ipswich)
G-BENF   Cessna T.210L   Spares

PARHAM
(Or Framlingham, on the B1116 north of Woodbridge)
N11024   Cessna 150L   Stored

WALPOLE
(On the B1117 south east of Halesworth) Blyth Valley Aviation Collection
WN907   7416M Hunter F.2   Nose
XL388   8750M Vulcan B.2A   Nose
XN696   Sea Vixen FAW.2   Nose
               Vampire T.11   Pod

WATTISHAM
WJ603   8664M Canberra B.2   Fire
XM192   8413M Lightning F.1A   Gate
XR718   8932M Lightning F.3   BDRT
XS922   Lightning F.6   BDRT
XT595   8851M Phantom FG.1   BDRT
                                    noseless
XV154   8854M Buccaneer S.2A   BDRT

WOODBRIDGE			25	Mystere IVA	Decoy
37414	F-4C-15-MC Phantom	BDRT	50	Mystere IVA	Decoy
70270	F-101B-80-MC Voodoo	BDRT	133	Mystere IVA	Decoy
9	Mystere IVA	Decoy	276	Mystere IVA	Decoy

Surrey

BANSTEAD
(On the A217 north of Reigate)

G-APZE	Apache 160	Wreck
G-ATLN	Cessna F.172G	Wreck
G-ATRD	Cessna F.150F	Wreck
G-AXXA	Cherokee 180E	Wreck
G-AZDB	Pup 100	Wreck
G-AZWU	Cessna F.150L	Wreck
G-BAXW	Cessna F.150L	Wreck

BROOKLANDS
(Or Weybridge) Brooklands Museum Not yet open to the public. Contact : Brooklands Museum, The Clubhouse, Brooklands Road, Weybridge, Surrey KT13 0QN. Telephone 0932 57381.

G-ADRY"	B'29 Mignet HM.14	Loan
G-AEKV	DZQ Kronfeld Drone	Loan
G-ANCF	Britannia 308F	Stored
G-BJHV	Voisin replica	Loan
G-LOTI	Bleriot XI replica	Loan
G-MJPB	Manuel Ladybird	Loan
G-VTOL	ZA250 Harrier T.52	-
BAPC 187	Roe I Biplane replica	-
BAPC 194	Demoiselle replica	Loan
BGA.643	ATH Gull III	Loan
	Curtiss Pusher rep	Loan
	Hols der Teufel	Loan
	Zlin Krajanek	Loan
A40-AB	VC-10 1103	-
D-12-354	Rheinland	Loan
B7270" G-BFCZ	Sopwith Camel rep	Restn
G1381" B'177	Avro 504K replica	Restn
L6906" B' 44	Magister I	Stored
N2980	Wellington 1A	Restn
XA292	Cadet TX.3	Loan
E-421 G-9-443	Hunter F.51	Inst
R4 BAPC 114	Vickers Viking replica	-

Brooklands Technical College

XJ772	Vampire T.11	Inst

BYFLEET

NP303 G-ANZJ	Proctor IV	Stored

CAMBERLEY
Various locations

G-AJUD	J/1 Autocrat	Restn
G-AYDW	Terrier 2	Restn
G-JETS	Terrier 2	Restn
XN493	Jet Provost T.3	Nose

CHARLWOOD
(West of Gatwick) Vallance Byways

G-JETH	XE489 Sea Hawk FB.5	-
VZ638	G-JETM Meteor T.7	-
WH903	8584M Canberra B.2	Nose
XE998	Vampire T.11	-
XP398	8794M Whirlwind HAR.10	-

Locally

E-430 G-9-448	Hunter F.51	-

DUNSFOLD

G-ARPZ	Trident 1C	Inst
WT488	Canberra T.4	Fire

EGHAM

XN435 G-BGBU	Auster AOP.9	Restn

FAIROAKS

G-GBCA	Agusta A.109	Travelling demonstrator
G-JGFF	AB.206B JetRanger	Wreck

GODALMING
1254 Squadron ATC, Hallam Road

WV332 G-9-406	Hunter F.4	Nose

REDHILL
Redhill Technical College

G-ANOA	Hiller UH-12A	Inst
G-AWTU	Musketeer A23-19A	Inst

East Surrey Technical College

G-KOOL	VP967 Sea Devon C.2	Inst

REDHILL AERODROME

G-ASYW	Bell 47G-2	Stored
G-AXGS	Condor	Stored
G-AYNP	Whirlwind Srs 3	Stored
G-TIGD	Super Puma	Wreck
5N-AJH G-ATLZ	Whirlwind Srs 3	Inst

REIGATE
Surrey Fire Brigade HQ

G-AWZI	Trident 3B-101	Fuselage

TONGHAM
(On the A3014 south of Aldershot)

G-AHUG	T'craft Plus D	Restn
G-AJAB	J/1N Alpha	Stored
G-ASEE	J/1N Alpha	Stored

VIRGINIA WATER
(On the A30 south west of Egham)
G-OILS   Cessna T.210L   -

WOKING
1349 Squadron ATC, Westfield Ave
XM697   Gnat T.1   -

East Sussex

HAILSHAM
Boship Barn Farm Hotel
G-AYOE   Bell 47G   Composite

HASTINGS
G-ACXE   L-25C-1 Swallow   Restn
WL345   Meteor T.7   Displayed

LEWES
G-APNS   Linnet   Restn

ROBERTSBRIDGE
(On the A21 north west of Hastings)
Robertsbridge Aviation Society   The
museum is open to the public every
Thursday evening from 1700 and on the
last Sunday afternoon of each month
except December.   Contact : Dennis
Woodgate, RAS, Cwmavon, Northbridge
Street, Robertsbridge, East Sussex,
TN32 5NY.
G-AIVW   Tiger Moth   Remains
WZ822   Grasshopper TX.1   -
                Horsa   Section

RYE
G-BAYL   Norecrin VI   Restn

ST LEONARDS-ON-SEA
BAPC 19   Bristol F.2b   Frame
D7889 G-AANM   Bristol F.2b   Restn
PV202 G-TRIX   Spitfire Tr IX   Restn

SEAFORD
G-BHNG   Aztec 250E   Fuselage

SEDLESCOMBE
(North of Hastings)
G-AWFT   Jodel D.9   Stored
G-AXPG   Mignet HM.293   Stored
F-BSIL   Cessna F.150K   Spares

UCKFIELD
2530 Squadron ATC, Headley Court
XP677   8587M Jet Provost T.4   Nose

West Sussex

CRAWLEY
XN334   A2525 SARO P.531   Restn

FAYGATE
(On the A264 between Horsham and
Crawley) Park Aviation Supply
G-BFTD   AA-5A Cheetah   Wreck
WH911   Canberra E.15   Nose
XG226   8800M Hunter F.6A   Nose
XP568   Jet Provost T.4   Fuse
XP976   Hawker P.1127   Hulk
XT459   Wessex HU.5   Wreck
XT866   Phantom FG.1   Wreck
XX114   Jaguar GR.1   Wreck
XX137   Jaguar T.2   Wreck
XX293   Hawk T.1   Wreck
XZ120   Jaguar GR.1   Wreck
XZ438   Sea Harrier FRS.1   Wreck
                F-4D Phantom II   Nose

GATWICK
Airport
G-APMB   Comet 4B   Cabin trainer
G-AWZX   Trident 3B-101   Dump
SX-BBD"G-BBBD Aztec 250E   Dump
Gatwick Hilton Hotel
G-AAAH" B'168 DH.60G Moth replica   -

SHOREHAM-BY-SEA
G-ALVP   Tiger Moth   Restn

SHOREHAM AIRPORT
G-AMNN"   Tiger Moth   Inst
G-AOIS   Tiger Moth   Restn
G-APNJ   Cessna 310   Inst
G-ARBO   Comanche 250   Restn
G-ARRM   Beagle 206-1X   Stored
G-ASFD   Morava L-200A   Stored
G-AVDF   Pup 200   Stored
G-AVUK   Enstrom F.28A/UK   Wreck
G-BDJP   J-3C-90 Cub   Stored

G-BJAP		Tiger Moth	Restn
G-BNPU	XL929	Pembroke C.1	Inst
		Tiger Moth	Frame
EC-AIU		Tiger Moth	Restn
VQ-SAC		BN-2A Islander	Nose
5N-AEE	G-AOJS	Chipmunk 22	Restn
5N-AGP	G-AOZU	Chipmunk 22	Restn

S L I N F O L D

G-AMKU		J/1B Aiglet	Stored
G-ARLO		Terrier 1	Spares
G-BBHJ		J-3C-65 Cub	Restn

T A N G M E R E

Tangmere Military Aviation Museum
The museum is open daily 1100 to 1730
from March 1 to early November.
Contact : Tangmere Military Aviation
Museum, PO Box 50, Tangmere Airfield,
Chichester, West Sussex PO20 6ER.
Telephone 0243 775223.

XF314"	E-412	Hunter F.51	-
19252		T-33A-1-LO	-
C4E-88		Bf 109E	Poor state

Tyne & Wear

G A T E S H E A D
Saltwell Park

G-WHIZ"G-AMOE	Viscount 701	Fuselage

N E W C A S T L E   A I R P O R T
(Or Woolsington)

G-ATSY	Super Baladou IV	Restn

S U N D E R L A N D
North East Aircraft Museum The museum
is open every day from 1100 to 1800.
During the winter period a 'phone call
to check times is advisable. Group
visits are welcome with prior notice.
Contact : North East Aircraft Museum,
Old Washington Road, Sunderland, Tyne
& Wear SR5 3HZ. Tel: 091 5813602.

G-ANFU		Auster 5	Stored
G-AWRS		Avro XIX Srs 2	-
G-SFTA		Gazelle 1	Cabin etc
BAPC 96		Brown Helicopter	-
BAPC 97		Luton LA-4 Minor	-
BAPC 119		Bensen B.7	-
RH746		Brigand TF.1	Fuselage
VX577		Valetta C.2	-
WA577	7718M	Sycamore 3	-
WB685		Chipmunk T.10	Loan
WD790	8743M	Meteor NF.11	Nose

WD889		Firefly AS.5	Composite
WG724		Dragonfly HR.5	-
WJ639		Canberra TT.18	-
WK198	7428M	Swift F.4	Fuselage
WL181		Meteor F.8	-
WL405		Meteor T.7	Noseless
WN516		Balliol T.2	Cockpit
WZ518		Vampire T.11	Composite
WZ767		Grasshopper TX.1	-
XG518	8009M	Sycamore HR.14	-
XG680		Sea Venom FAW.22	Restn
XL319		Vulcan B.2A	-
XM660		Whirlwind HAS.7	-
XP627		Jet Provost T.4	-
XW276		Gazelle 03	-
ZF594	53-696	Lightning F.53	-
		Comet 4	Nose
		Canberra	Nose
		Auster AOP.6	Frame
		Sycamore HR.14	Nose
146		Mystere IVA	-
E-419	G-9-441	Hunter F.51	-
42157		F-100D-16-NA S'Sabre	-
54439		T-33A-1-LO	-
171	51-6171	F-86D-35-NA Sabre	-
541	52-6541	F-84F-40-RE T'streak	-
2214 Squadron ATC			
XD622	8160M	Vampire T.11	-

Warwickshire

C O V E N T R Y   A I R P O R T
(Or Baginton) Midland Air Museum
MAM is open from April (or Easter if
it is in March) to October, Mondays to
Fridays 1000-1600, Sundays and Bank
Holidays 1100-1800. November to March
Sundays only 1100-1800 or dusk (except
Christmas).   Contact : Midland Air

Museum, Baginton, Coventry, CV8 3AZ -
please enclose SAE. Tel: 0203 301033.

G-EBJG	Pixie III	Stored
G-ABOI	Wheeler Slymph	Stored
G-AEGV	Mignet HM.14	Stored
G-ALCU	Dove 2	-
G-APJJ	Fairey Ultralight	-

G-APRL		Argosy 101	-
G-APWN		Whirlwind Srs 3	-
G-BAPC		Luton LA.4 Minor	Stored
G-SHIP		Aztec 250F	-
BAPC 32		Crossley Tom Thumb	
			Stored
BAPC 67		Bf 109 replica	Stored
BAPC 126		Turbulent	-
VP-KJL	G-ALAR	Messenger 4A	Stored
H3426"	B'68	Hurricane replica	Stored
EE531	7090M	Meteor F.4	-
VF301	7060M	Vampire F.1	-
VM325		Anson C.19	-
VS623	G-AOKZ	Prentice T.1	-
VT935		BP-111A	-
WF922		Canberra PR.3	-
WS838		Meteor NF.14	-
WV797	A2637	Sea Hawk FGA.6	-
XA508	A2472	Gannet T.2	-
XA699	7809M	Javelin FAW.5	-
XA862	A2542	Whirlwind HAS.1	-
XD626		Vampire T.11	-
XE855		Vampire T.11	Stored
XE872		Vampire T.11	Stored
XF382		Hunter F.6A	-
XK741		Gnat T.1	Fuselage
XK907		Whirlwind HAS.7	Stored
XL360		Vulcan B.2A	-
XN691	8143M	Sea Vixèn FAW.2	Stored, on loan
XR771		Lightning F.6	Loan
ZF598	55-713	Lightning T.55	-
E-425	G-9-446	Hunter F.51	-
R-756		F-104G Starfighter	-
14419		T-33A-1-LO	-
42174		F-100D-16-NA S'Sabre	-
70		Mystere IVA	-
24535		HH-43B Huskie	-
82062		U-6A Beaver	-
28368		Fl 282V-20 Kolibri	Frame
29640		3AAB J.29F Tunnan	-

Aircraft Radio Museum and Percival Collection Contact : John F Coggins, Aircraft Radio Museum, Baginton, Coventry, Warwickshire.

G-AMLZ	Prince 6E	-
G-AOKO	Prentice 1	Spares
G-APJB	Prentice 1	-

Airport

G-ASUS		MJ.2B Tempete	Stored
G-AYKZ		SAI KZ-8	Stored
G-AWSH	"G-ASWH	Luton LA.5 Major	Stored
CS-ACQ		Fleet 80 Canuck	Stored
37		Nord 3400	Stored

39		Nord 3400	Stored
68		Nord 3400	Stored
121		Nord 3400	Stored
124	G-BOSJ	Nord 3400	Stored
114700		T-6G-NH Texan	Stored
151632	"N9494Z	TB-25N-NC	Stored
N9+AA"	G-BECL	CASA 352L	Stored

LAWFORD HEATH
(Near Church Lawford) 8 Group, ROC, Industrial Estate

WT651	7532M	Hunter F.1	Gate

LONG MARSTON
Stratford Aircraft Collection
Enquiries : 32 Flaxley Close, Winyates Green, Redditch, Worcs, B98 0QS.

BAPC 200		Bensen B.8	Loan
VR200	G-APIU	Prentice T.1	-
WB624		Chipmunk T.10	Loan, fuselage
WN739	G-TACA	Sea Prince T.1	-
WT483		Canberra T.4	-
WZ798		Grasshopper TX.1	-
XA293		Cadet TX.3	-
XD447		Vampire T.11	-
XJ575		Sea Vixen FAW.2	Nose
XP346	8793M	Whirlwind HAR.10	-
XT242		Sioux AH.1	Loan

Airfield

		Cessna Para-trainer	
XG692		Sea Venom FAW.21	Stored

NUNEATON
Scrapyard, Attleborough Road

G-BHCR	PC.6-B2/H2	Wreck

WARWICK

SX300	A2054	Seafire F.17	Stored

WELLESBOURNE MOUNTFORD
Wellesbourne Aviation Group Contact : Dell Paddock, 2 Longford Close, Bidford-on-Avon, Alcester, Warks, B50 4EB. Telephone 0789 778816.

XK590		Vampire T.11	-

Others

XM655	G-VULC	Vulcan B.2A	Stored

Wiltshire

BOSCOMBE DOWN

G-ALRX	Britannia 101	Nose
FS890	7554M Harvard IIB	Spares
VP968	Devon C.2/2	Dump
VZ345	Sea Fury T.20S	Restn
WH876	Canberra B.2(mod)	Stored
WT309	Canberra B(I).6	Stored
XL472	Gannet AEW.3	Inst
XL629	Lightning T.4	Gate
XL898	8654M Whirlwind HAR.9	Inst
XN923	Buccaneer S.1	Test rig
XR773	Lightning F.6	Stored
XV784	8909M Harrier GR.3	Nose
	Canberra B.6	Nose

CHILMARK
(South of the A303 between Wylye and Cricklade)

XP140	8806M Wessex HAS.3	Inst

CORSHAM
HMS Royal Arthur

XN302	A2654 Whirlwind HAS.7	Inat

CRUDWELL
(On the A429 south of Kemble) Scrapyard

XK912	Whirlwind HAS.7	-

KEEVIL

WZ620	Vampire T.11	Stored
XE921	Vampire T.11	Stored

LYNEHAM

XJ676	8844M Hunter F.6A	Dump
XK699	7971M Comet C.2	Gate
XL445	8811M Vulcan K.2	Dump

MARLBOROUGH
2293 Squadron ATC, London Road

	Chipmunk T.10	PAX tnr

MONKTON FARLEIGH
(East of the A363, east of Bath) Avon Air Museum at Monkton Farleigh Mines. Contact : 8 Hobbes Close, Malmesbury, Wilts, SN16 0DA.

WF825	8359M Meteor T.7	-
XE849	7928M Vampire T.11	-
XH767	7955M Javelin FAW.9	-

NETHERAVON

G-BBRP	BN-2A-9 Islander	Para-trainer
XP827	Beaver AL.1	Fire
XT470	Wessex HU.5	Fire

SALISBURY
Hampshire Light Plane Services

G-ADMT	Hornet Moth	Restn
G-ADPR	Gull Six	Restn
G-AEDU	N190DH DH.90 Dragonfly	Restn
G-AEZJ	Vega Gull	Restn
G-AHUN	GC-1B Swift	Restn
EC-ADE	Moth Major	Frame

TROWBRIDGE

XV372	SH-3D Sea King	Scrapyard

UPAVON

G-AIGF	J/1N Alpha	Stored

WARMINSTER

G-AJIS	J/1N Alpha	Restn

WINTERBOURNE GUNNER
(On the A338 north of Salisbury) Nuclear, Bacteriological & Chemical Defence Centre

XK531	8403M Buccaneer S.1	Inst
XR478	Whirlwind HAR.10	Inst
XR482	Whirlwind HAR.10	Inst
XT430	Wasp HAS.1	Inst

WROUGHTON
Science Museum Air Transport Collection and Storage Facility
Details of events planned at Wroughton can be had from : The Science Museum, South Kensington, London SW7 2DD. 01 938 8000.

G-AACN	HP Gugnunc	-
G-ACIT	DH.84 Dragon	-
G-AEHM	Mignet HM.14	-
G-ALXT	Dragon Rapide	-
G-APWY	Piaggio P.166	-
G-APYD	Comet 4B	-
G-AVYE	Trident 1E	For disposal
G-AVZB	Z37 Cmelak	-
G-AWZM	Trident 3B-101	-
G-MMCB	Huntair Pathfinder	-
G-RBOS	Colt AS-105	-
BAPC 162	Newbury Manflier	Major parts
BAPC 172	Chargus Midas	-
BAPC 173	Birdman Grasshopper	-
BAPC 174	Bensen B.7	-
BAPC 188	McBroom Cobra 88	-
EI-AYO	DC-3A-197	-
NC5171N	G-LIOA Lockheed 10A	-
N18E	Boeing 247	-
N7777G	G-CONI L-749A-79	-
VP975	Devon C.2/2	-

XD163	8645M	Whirlwind HAR.10	Stored
XG900		Short SC.1	-

Fleet Air Arm Museum Storage Facility

VH127		Firefly TT.4	-
WP313		Sea Prince T.1	-
WS103		Meteor T.7	-
XA129		Sea Vampire T.22	-
XA466		Gannet COD.4	-
XA864		Whirlwind HAR.1	-
XN332	A2579	SARO P.531	-
XN385		Whirlwind HAS.7	-
XS881	A2675	Wessex HAS.1	-
AE-422		UH-1H Iroquois	-

Royal Naval Aircraft Yard

XK911	A2603	Whirlwind HAS.7	Stored
XM916		Wessex HAS.3	Dump
XP190		Scout AH.1	Spares
XP850		Scout AH.1	Spares
XP855		Scout AH.1	Stored
XP890		Scout AH.1	Spares
XP893		Scout AH.1	Stored
XP902		Scout AH.1	Stored
XP903		Scout AH.1	Spares
XP909		Scout AH.1	Stored
XR595		Scout AH.1	Stored
XR602		Scout AH.1	Stored
XR627		Scout AH.1	Stored
XR628		Scout AH.1	Stored
XR629		Scout AH.1	Spares
XR630		Scout AH.1	Stored
XR632		Scout AH.1	Stored
XR637		Scout AH.1	Spares
XR639		Scout AH.1	Spares
XS120	8653M	Wessex HAS.1	Dump
XT616		Scout AH.1	Spares
XT617		Scout AH.1	Stored
XT623		Scout AH.1	Stored
XT626		Scout AH.1	Stored

XT633	Scout AH.1	Stored
XT637	Scout AH.1	Spares
XT639	Scout AH.1	Spares
XT642	Scout AH.1	Spares
XT643	Scout AH.1	Stored
XT645	Scout AH.1	Spares
XT648	Scout AH.1	Stored
XV118	Scout AH.1	Stored
XV119	Scout AH.1	Stored
XV121	Scout AH.1	Stored
XV123	Scout AH.1	Stored
XV124	Scout AH.1	Stored
XV131	Scout AH.1	Stored
XV138	Scout AH.1	Stored
XW281	Scout AH.1	Stored
XW284	Scout AH.1	Spares
XW616	Scout AH.1	Stored
XW795	Scout AH.1	Stored
XW796	Scout AH.1	Stored
XW846	Gazelle AH.1	Stored
XW893	Gazelle AH.1	Stored
XX378	Gazelle AH.1	Stored
XX392	Gazelle AH.1	Stored
XX399	Gazelle AH.1	Stored
XZ290	Gazelle AH.1	Stored
XZ320	Gazelle AH.1	Stored
XZ324	Gazelle AH.1	Stored
XZ326	Gazelle AH.1	Stored
XZ340	Gazelle AH.1	Stored
XZ671	Lynx AH.1	Stored
ZB676	Gazelle AH.1	Stored
ZB691	Gazelle AH.1	Stored
ZB692	Gazelle AH.1	Stored
ZB693	Gazelle AH.1	Stored
AE-520	CH-47C Chinook	Stored

Princess Alexandra Royal Air Force Hospital

WJ676	7796M	Canberra B.2	Gate

North Yorkshire

C A T T E R I C K
Royal Air Force Fire Fighting and Safety School

VP971	8824M	Devon C.2/2	-
WH794	8652M	Canberra PR.7	-
WH925		Canberra B.2	Nose
WJ867	8643M	Canberra T.4	-
WT362		Canberra B(I).8	Nose
XA939		Victor B(K).1A	Nose
XM997		Lightning T.4	Poor
XN652	8817M	Sea Vixen D.3	Poor
XN925	8087M	Buccaneer S.1	-

C H O P   G A T E
(On the B1257 north of Helmsley)
North Yorks Aircraft Recovery Centre

WM145	Meteor NF.11	Nose
WZ557	Vampire T.11	-
XN600	Jet Provost T.4	Nose

C H U R C H   F E N T O N

		Spitfire replica	Gate
XN473	8862M	Jet Provost T.3A	Nose

ELVINGTON
(Off the A1079 south east of York)
Yorkshire Air Museum and Allied Air
Forces Memorial   Open weekends and
Bank Holidays only between May and
September,   Saturdays   1400-1700,
Sundays and Bank Holidays 1100-1700.
Weekdays and evenings can be arranged
by prior appointment.   Contact :
Yorkshire Air Museum, Elvington, York,
YO4 5AT. Telephone : 0904 85 595.

F943"	G-BKDT	SE.5A replica	–
HJ711		Mosquito NF.II	Fuselage
HR792		Halifax II	Complex composite, restn
WH846		Canberra T.4	–
XD453	7890M	Vampire T.11	–
XS903		Lightning F.6	–

KIRKBYMOORSIDE

G-BECE	AD-500 Skyship	Gondola
G-BIUZ	T-67B	Static test
c/n 2006	T-67	Static test

LEEMING

WS844" WS788	Meteor NF.14	For disposal
XA634 7641M	Javelin FAW.4	Gate
XR753	Lightning F.6	BDRT

LINTON-ON-OUSE

XF545 7957M	Provost T.1	Gate

MARKINGTON
(West of the A61 south of Ripon)

G-AZII	SAN D.117A	Stored

SHERBURN-IN-ELMET

G-WYMP	Cessna F.150J	Wreck
F-BHDT G-BHCW	TriPacer 150	Stored

SUTTON-ON-THE-FOREST
(On the A1363 north of York)

XP749	Lightning F.3	Stored
XP750	Lightning F.3	Stored
XP764	Lightning F.3	Stored
XR720	Lightning F.3	Stored

South Yorkshire

ARMTHORPE
(On the A630 north of Doncaster)   1053
Squadron ATC

WG419	8206M	Chipmunk T.10	PAX tnr

ECCLESFIELD
(North of Sheffield)

WP255	Vampire NF.10	Pod

FINNINGLEY

WK864"	WL168	Meteor F.8	Gate
XJ729	8732M	Whirlwind HAR.10	Inst
XP404	8682M	Whirlwind HAR.10	Inst
XS216		Jet Provost T.4	Fuse
XV263	8967M	Nimrod AEW.3	Inst
XX297	8933M	Hawk T.1A	Fire
XX477	8462M	Jetstream T.1	Cockpit

ROSSINGTON
(On the A638 north of Bawtry) Central
Bottling Company

XR725	Lightning F.6	Stored
XR726	Lightning F.6	Stored
XR747	Lightning F.6	Stored
XR757	Lightning F.6	Stored
XR759	Lightning F.6	Stored
XS416	Lightning T.5	Stored
XS419	Lightning T.5	Stored
XS897	Lightning F.6	Stored
XS932	Ligthning F.6	Stored
XS935	Lightning F.6	Stored

ROTHERHAM

XH563	8744M	Vulcan B.2MRR	Nose

SHEFFIELD

BAPC 13	Mignet HM.14	Restn

West Yorkshire

B I N G L E Y

Auto Spares (Bingley) Ltd, Walsh Lane

WM705	Vampire NF.10	Pod
WM712	Vampire NF.10	Pod
WM714	Vampire NF.10	Pod
WM727	Vampire NF.10	Pod
WM730	Vampire NF.10	Pod
WP232	Vampire NF.10	Pod
WP239	Vampire NF.10	Pod
WP242	Vampire NF.10	Pod

D E W S B U R Y

Northern Aeroplane Workshops   Contact
: Northern Aeroplane Workshops, F W
Found, 7 Scoton Drive, Knaresborough,
North Yorks.

G-BOCK	Sopwith Triplane	Under construction
	Bristol M.1D Mono	Under construction

D R I G H L I N G T O N

(On the A58 south west of Leeds)

XG540	8345M Sycamore HR.14	-
XJ380	8628M Sycamore HR.14	-

E L L A N D

(On the A6026 between Halifax and
Huddersfield)

XK659	Comet C.2R	Nose

L E E D S

Anne Lindsay and Nigel Ponsford
Collection

G-AEFG BAPC75	Mignet HM.14	-
G-ARIF	OH-7 Coupe	Restn
BGA.491	Dagling	Stored
BAPC 14	Addyman STG	-
BAPC 16	Addyman Ultra-Light	-
BAPC 18	Killick MPA Gyroplane	-
BAPC 39	Addyman Zephyr	-
	Hutter H.17a	Stored
	Dickson Primary	Restn
RA848	Cadet TX.1	Nose
	Bristol F.2b	Frame

L E E D S - B R A D F O R D A I R P O R T

(Or Yeadon)

G-ACGT	Avian IIIA	Restn, locally
G-ATND	Cessna F.150F	Test-rig
G-AVGG	Cherokee 140	Spares
G-AWES	Cessna 150H	Wreck
G-AXZJ	Cessna F.172H	Restn

S I D D A L

(On the A646 south of Halifax)
Scrapyard

XG597	Whirlwind HAS.7	-
XH587	Victor K.1A	Nose
XL868 A2595	Whirlwind HAS.7	-
XM663	Whirlwind HAS.7	-
XT774	Wessex HU.5	-

Part 2

SCOTLAND – Central

C A U S E W A Y H E A D
(North of Stirling)
XG504	Sycamore HR.14	Scrapyard

Dumfries & Galloway

T I N W A L D   D O W N S
Dumfries & Galloway Aviation Group
(Off the A701 north west of Dumfries on the former airfield) The Museum is open to the public every Saturday and Sunday April to September from 1000-1700. Other times by appointment. Contact : 11 Ninian Court, Lochside, Dumfries.

P7540		Spitfire IIA	Remains
WA576	7900M	Sycamore 3	-
WJ903		Varsity T.1	Nose

WL375		Meteor T.7(mod)	-
XD425		Vampire T.11	-
		Vampire	Pod
		Venom	Pod
		Gannet	Fuselage
42163		F-100D-11-NA S'Sabre	-
FT-36		T-33A-1-LO	-
318		Mystere IVA	-

W E S T   F R E U G H
VP977	Devon C.2/2	Dump
XN817	Argosy C.1	Dump

Fife

C U P A R
XE802	Cadet TX.3	Stored

L E U C H A R S
WP320		Sea Prince T.1	Fire
XM144	8417M	Lightning F.1A	Gate
XM169	8422M	Lightning F.1A	Decoy

XM178	8418M	Lightning F.1A	Decoy
XN781	8538M	Lightning F.2A	Decoy
XR713	8935M	Lightning F.3	Gate
XR749	8934M	Lightning F.3	BDRT
XT857	8913M	Phantom FG.1	Inst
XV588		Phantom FG.1	BDRT
XV591		Phantom FG.1	WLT

Grampian

A B E R D E E N
Grampian Fire Brigade HQ, Anderson Dr
VR-BBN	G-AOYB	Whirlwind Srs 3	Inst

A B E R D E E N   A I R P O R T
(Or Dyce)
G-ARPN		Trident 1	Fire crews
N64P	G-ASTD	Aztec 250C	Dump
N150JC		Bonanza A35	Restn

A B O Y N E
G-BALK	SNCAN SV-4C	Restn

K I N L O S S
G-BDIU	8882M	Comet 4C	Section
VV950		Anson T.21	Wreck
XW549	8860M	Buccaneer S.2B	BDR

L O S S I E M O U T H
WL738	8567M	Shackleton MR.2C	Gate
WL798	8114M	Shackleton MR.2C	Spares
WR967	8398M	Shackleton MR.2C	Fuse
XG882	8754M	Gannet T.5	Gate
XK532	8867M	Buccaneer S.1	Gate
XL609	8866M	Hunter T.7	BDRT
XN929	8051M	Buccaneer S.1	Nose
XT281	8705M	Buccaneer S.2B	WLT

Highlands

EDDERTON
(On the A9 north west of Tain)

G-ASEU	D.62A Condor	Restn
G-AVKM	D.62B Condor	Spares
c/n 180 Pup		Fuselage

TAIN

XG731	Sea Venom FAW.22	Poor

The Islands

ORPHIR
(Near Kirkwall, Orkney)

G-ASRP	SAN DR.1050	Stored

STORNOWAY AIRPORT
(Isle of Lewis)

G-GUNN	Cessna F.172H	Fire

SUMBURGH AIRPORT
(Shetland)

F-BMCY	Potez 840	Fire

Lothian

EAST FORTUNE
Royal Museum of Scotland - Museum of Flight Open 1000-1600 all week during July and August. Beyond this period prior application should be made. contact : Museum of Flight, East Fortune Airfield, North Berwick, East Lothian, EH39 5LF. Tel 062 088 308.

G-ACYK		Spartan Cruiser	Section
G-AGBN		Cygnet II	-
G-ANOV		Dove 6	-
G-ARCX	WM261	Meteor 14	-
G-ASUG		Beech D.18S	-
G-ATOY		Comanche 260B	Wreck
G-AXEH		Bulldog 1	-
G-BBVF	XM961	Twin Pioneer 2	-
G-BDFU		Dragonfly II MPA	-
G-BDIX	XR399	Comet 4C	-
G-BIRW		MS.505 Criquet	-
VH-SNB		Dragon I	-
VH-UQB	G-ABDW	Puss Moth	-
BGA 852	TS291	T.8 Tutor	-
BGA 902		Gull I	-
BGA1014		T.21B	-
W-2	BAPC 85	Weir W-2	-
BAPC 12		Mignet HM.14	Loan
BAPC160		Chargus 18/50	-
BAPC195		Moonraker 77	-
BAPC196		Sigma IIM	-
BAPC197		Cirrus 3	-
N9510	G-AOEL	Tiger Moth	-
TE462	7243M	Spitfire XVI	-

VM360	G-APHV	Anson C.19	-
WF259	A2483	Sea Hawk F.2	-
WV493	G-BDYG	Provost T.1	-
WW145		Sea Venom FAW.22	-
XA109		Sea Vampire T.22	-
XL762	8017M	Skeeter AOP.12	-
XM597		Vulcan B.2A	-
XN776		Lightning F.2A	-
591		Rhonlerche II	-
9940		Bolingbroke IVT	-
		WACO CG-4A	Nose
191659		Me 163B-1a	-

Aircraft Preservation Society of Scotland Contact : Aircraft Preservation Society of Scotland, c/o Museum of Flight, East Fortune Airfield, North Berwick, East Lothian, EH39 5LF.

G-AFJU		Miles Monarch	Restn
G-ARTJ		Bensen B.8M	-
G-ATFG		Brantly B.2B	-
TJ398"	BAPC70	Auster AOP.6	-

EDINBURGH
Royal Museum of Scotland, Chambers Street. Open Monday to Saturday 1000-1700 and Sunday 1400-1700. Contact : Royal Museum of Scotland, Chambers Street, Edinburgh, EH1 1JF. Tel 031 225 7534.

BAPC 49	Pilcher Hawk	-

E D I N B U R G H   A I R P O R T
(Or Turnhouse)
| G-ARPL | Trident 1C | Fire |
| | Spitfire replica | Gate |

Strathclyde

B E A R S D E N
(North of Glasgow)
| G-AXBU | Cessna FR.172F | Wreck |

D U N O O N
2296 Squadron ATC
| WZ866 | 8217M Chipmunk T.10 | PAX tnr |

G L A S G O W   A I R P O R T
(Or Abbotsinch)
G-ARPP		Trident 1C	Fire
G-ATJC		Airtourer 100	Stored
G-BIUU		Aztec 250D	Spares
G-SEAB		RC-3 Seabee	Restn
N6037	G-ANNB	Tiger Moth	Restn
N9467T		Tomahawk	Restn
J-1614	G-BLIE	Venom FB.50	Stored

H O L L Y B U S H
(On the A713 south east of Ayr)
| G-ANNN | Tiger Moth | Stored |

K I L K E R R A N
| G-AIGU | J/1N Alpha | Restn |
| G-AREH | Tiger Moth | Stored |

K I L M A R N O C K
327 Squadron ATC, Aird Avenue
WB584	7706M Chipmunk T.10	PAX tnr
WJ872	8492M Canberra T.4	Nose
	Hunter	Nose

M A C H R I H A N I S H
| WL635 | | Varsity T.1 | Dog School |
| XL427 | 8756M | Vulcan B.2A | Dump |

P R E S T W I C K   A I R P O R T
G-ATDB	Noralpha	Stored
G-ATXJ	Jetstream '41'	Mock-up
G-AWZJ	Trident 3B-101	Fire
	Jetstream 200	Rig
XL497	Gannet AEW.3	Gate
XX660	Bulldog T.1	Sectioned

Tayside

A R B R O A T H
| TX183 | Anson C.19 | Restn |

D U N D E E   A I R P O R T
(Or Riverside)
| G-ASAI | Airedale | Restn |
| G-BDOW | FRA.150M Aerobat | Wreck |

M O N T R O S E
Offshore Petroleum Industry Training
Board
| XJ723 | Whirlwind HAR.10 | Inst |

P E R T H   A I R P O R T
(Or Scone) Scottish Aircraft
Collection Trust SACT, Tillywhally,
Milnathort, Tayside. Tel 0577 63326.
G-AHKY		Miles M.18 Srs 2	-
VS356	G-AOLU	Prentice T.1	-
VZ728	G-AGOS	Desford Trainer	-

Air Service Training
G-ALWS	Tiger Moth	-
G-ARBC	Cessna 310D	Inst
G-ARPX	Trident 1C	Inst
G-ARTX	Cessna 150B	Fuselage
G-ARTY	Cessna 150B	Inst
G-ATNJ	Cessna F.150F	Inst
G-ATOF	Cessna F.150F	Inst
G-ATOG	Cessna F.150F	Inst
G-AVDB	Cessna 310L	Inst
G-AYBW	Cessna FA.150K	Inst
G-AYGB	Cessna 310Q	Inst
G-BBCF	Cessna FRA.150L	Fuselage
G-BEWP	Cessna F.150M	Inst
F-BGNR	Viscount 708	Inst
WW453	Provost T.1	Inst
XL875	Whirlwind HAR.9	Inst
XT140	Sioux AH.1	Inst
XX467	Hunter T.7	Inst
	Chipmunk T.10	Inst

Others
| G-AOFJ | Auster 5 | Restn |

S T R A T H A L L A N
Strathallan Aircraft Collection
Open April to October daily 1000-
1700. Contact : Strathallan Aircraft
Collection, Strathallan Airfield,
Auchterarder, Tayside, PH3 1LA. Tel
07646 2545.

G-ACVA		Kay Gyroplane	–
G-ANOK		SAAB Safir	–
G-AYWA		Avro XIX Srs 2	Restn
G-BEPV		Fokker S.11-1	–

BAPC 170		Pilcher Hawk replica	–
F5447"	G-BKER	Scale SE.5A	Airworthy
R1914	G-AHUJ	Magister I	–
V9441"	G-AZWT	Lysander III	Airworthy
W5856	G-BMGC	Swordfish II	Restn
VP293		Shackleton T.4	–
XD547		Vampire T.11	Pod, loan
XE340		Sea Hawk FGA.6	–
XE897"	XD403	Vampire T.11	–
XG594		Whirlwind HAS.7	–
XK655	G-AMXA	Comet C.2R-	
		Fokker D.VI replica	–
		Fokker D.VII replica	–

Part 3

WALES – Clwyd

C H E S T E R   A I R P O R T
(Or Hawarden, or Broughton)

G-ARYA	HS.125-1	Nose
TZ-ADT	BAe 146-100	Stored
G-ASSM	HS.125-1	Restn
XN685	8173M Sea Vixen FAW.2	Inst

C H I R K

G-AIUL	Dragon Rapide	Stored
G-AJBJ	Dragon Rapide	Stored
G-AKOE	Dragon Rapide	Stored
G-ASBU	Terrier 2	Spares
G-BDAO	SIPA 91	Stored
G-BEDB	Norecrin	Stored

C O N N A H ' S   Q U A Y
(On the A548 west of Chester) North Wales Institute of Higher Education

G-APMY	Apache 160	Inst
G-AZMX	Cherokee 140	Inst
XA460	Gannet AS.4	Inst

H A W A R D E N
(On the A55 south west of Chester) 2247 Squadron ATC, Manor Lane

XE852	Vampire T.11	

S E A L A N D

XF979"	8565M Hunter F.51	Gate

Dyfed

A B E R P O R T H

WT680	7533M Hunter F.1	1429 Sqn ATC

B R A W D Y

XE624	8875M Hunter FGA.9	Gate
XF435	8880M Hunter FGA.9	BDRT
XL728	Wessex HAS.1	Dump

H A V E R F O R D W E S T
(Or Withybush)

G-AWKM	Pup 100	Spares
XK378	TA200 Auster AOP.9	Stored

L L A N E L L I

G-AHTE	Proctor V	Restn

P E N D I N E   R A N G E S
(On the A4066 east of Tenby)

WH844	Canberra T.4	–
XA938	Victor K.1	Fuselage
XD241	Scimitar F.1	–
XF439	8712M Hunter F.6A	–
XG138"	Hunter	–
XJ411	Whirlwind HAR.10	–
XK536	Buccaneer S.1	–
XM139	8411M Lightning F.1A	–
XM147	8412M Lightning F.1A	–
XM299	Wessex HC.2	–
XM926	Wessex HAS.1	–
XN926	Buccaneer S.1	–
XN933	Buccaneer S.1	–
XN965	Buccaneer S.1	–
XP735	Lightning F.3	–
XR479	Whirlwind HAR.10	–
XV338	Buccaneer S.2	–
XV340	8659M Buccaneer S.2	–

Mid Glamorgan

B R I D G E N D
(On the A473 west of Cardiff) 192 Squadron ATC, TAVR Centre

G-AOHR	Viscount 802	Nose

K E N F I G   H I L L
(North of the B4281 east of Pyle) 2117 Squadron ATC, Main Street

WT569	7491M Hunter F.1	–

South Glamorgan

CARDIFF - WALES AIRPORT

(Or Rhoose) Wales Aircraft Museum WAM is open daily June to September from 1000 to 1800. October to May it is open Saturdays 1100 to dusk and Sundays 1400 to dusk. Contact : Gwyn Roberts, 19 Clos Glyndwr, Hendy, Dyfed, SA4 1FW. Tel 0792 883451.

G-AOJC	Viscount 802	-
G-ARBY"G-ANRS	Viscount 732	Fuselage
WB491	Avro Ashton	Nose
WE925	Meteor F.8	Composite
WG718 A2531	Dragonfly HR.3	-
WH798 8130M	Canberra PR.7	Fuselage
WJ576	Canberra T.17	-
WJ944	Varsity T.1	-
WL332	Meteor T.7	-
WM292	Meteor TT.20	-
WR539 8399M	Venom FB.4	-
WT518 8691M	Canberra PR.7	-
WV753 8113M	Pembroke C.1	-
WV826 A2532	Sea Hawk FGA.6	-
WW388 7616M	Provost T.1	-
WX788	Venom NF.3	-
WZ425	Vampire T.11	-
WZ826" XD826	Valiant BK.1	Nose
XA459 A2608	Gannet AS.4	-
XA903	Vulcan B.1	Nose
XF383" E-409	Hunter F.51	-
XG592	Whirlwind HAS.7	-
XG737	Sea Venom FAW.22	-
XG883	Gannet T.5	-
XH177	Canberra PR.9	Nose
XJ409	Whirlwind HAR.10	-
XL449	Gannet AEW.3	-
XM300	Wessex HAS.1	-
XM569	Vulcan B.2A	-
XN650 A2639	Sea Vixen FAW.2	-
XN928 8179M	Buccaneer S.1	-
ZF578 53-670	Lightning F.53	-
29963	T-33A-1-LO	-
42160	F-100D-16-NA S'Sabre	-
59	Mystere IVA	-

Airport

G-AOJE	Viscount 802	Fire
G-SEXY	AA-1 Yankee	Stored
G-BGSS	Tomahawk 112	Cockpit

ST ATHAN

Historic Aircraft Collection Collection no longer open to the public and in the process of wind-down. Most airframes will be going to Cosford. Contact :Officer in Charge, RAF St Athan

Historic Aircraft Collection, RAF St Athan, Barry, South Glamorgan, CF6 9WA. Tel 04465 3131.

G-AEEH		HM.14 Pou du Ciel	-
BAPC.47		Watkins CHW	-
BAPC.83 8476M		Ki 100-1b	-
BAPC.92		Fi 103 (V1)	-
6232" BAPC.41		BE.2c replica	Travelling exhibit
H1968"BAPC.42		Avro 504K rep	Travelling exhibit
L5343		Battle I	Restn
Z7197	8380M	Proctor III	-
EE549	7008M	Meteor IV Special	-
MK356	5690M	Spitfire IX	-
TJ138	7607M	Mosquito TT.35	-
WD935	8440M	Canberra B.2	-
WE600	7602M	Auster C4	-
WK281	7712M	Swift FR.5	-
WL505	7705M	Vampire FR.9	-
WS843	7937M	Meteor NF.14	-
WV499	7698M	Provost T.1	-
XM602	8771M	Vulcan B.2A	-
XN341	8022M	Skeeter AOP.12	-
XR243	8057M	Auster AOP.9	-
XR486	8727M	Whirlwind HCC.12	-
XS650	8801M	Swallow TX.1	-
112372	8482M	Me 262A-2a	-
120227	8472M	He 162A-2	-
420430	8483M	Me 410A-1/U2	-
475081	7362M	Fi 156C-7	-
584219	8470M	Fw 190F-8/U1	-
5439	BAPC.84	Mitsubishi Ki 46	-

St Athan Maintenance Unit abd other locations. CTTS = Civilian Technical Training School.

PK664	7759M	Spitfire F.22	Stored
VP958	8795M	Devon C.2/2	For disposal
WH780		Canberra T.22	Stored
WH797		Canberra T.22	Stored
WH801		Canberra T.22	Stored
WH803		Canberra T.22	Stored
WH984	8101M	Canberra B.15	Nose, CTTS
WJ574		Canberra TT.18	Stored
WJ717		Canberra TT.18	Stored
WJ861		Canberra T.4	Stored
WK144	8689M	Canberra B.2	Dump
WT510		Canberra T.22	Stored
WT525		Canberra T.22	Stored
WT535		Canberra T.22	Stored
WT648	7530M	Hunter F.1	Dump
XA243	8886M	Grasshopper TX.1	Inst
XE793	8666M	Cadet TX.3	Inst
XF526	8679M	Hunter F.6	Stored
XG154	8863M	Hunter FGA.9	Stored
XH133		Canberra PR.9	Stored
XH165		Canberra PR.9	Stored

XL163	8916M	Victor K.2	Dump
XL578		Hunter T.7	Stored
XL595		Hunter T.7	Stored
XN458	8334M	Jet Provost T.3	CTTS
XN632	8352M	Jet Provost T.3	CTTS
XP502	8576M	Gnat T.1	CTTS
XP542	8575M	Gnat T.1	CTTS
XP558	8627M	Jet Provost T.4	CTTS
XP680	8460M	Jet Provost T.4	CTTS
XR541	8602M	Gnat T.1	CTTS
XV156	8773M	Buccaneer S.2A	Dump
XX635	8767M	Bulldog T.1	CTTS
XW545	8859M	Buccaneer S.2B	BDRT
XW550		Buccaneer S.2B	Stored

Gwent

C W M B R A N
(South of Newport) <u>2308 Squadron ATC</u>,
Greenhill Road

WD293	7645M	Chipmunk T.10	PAX tnr

Gwynedd

C A E R N A R F O N   A I R P O R T
(Or Llandwrog) <u>Snowdon Mountain
Aviation & Museum</u> Enquiries should be
made to :- Snowdon Mountain Aviation,
Caernarfon Airport, Llandwrog,
Caernarfon, Gwynedd, LL54 5TP. Tel
0286 830800.

G-AIDL		Dragon Rapide 6	A/w
G-ALFT		Dove 6	-
		Mignet HM.14	-
TX235		Anson C.19	-
WN499		Dragonfly HR.3	-
WV781	7839M	Sycamore HR.12	-
XA282		Cadet TX.3	-
XD599	G-VAMP"	Vampire T.11	-
XH837	8032M	Javelin FAW.7	Nose
XJ726		Whirlwind HAR.10	-
XK623		Vampire T.11	-

L L A N B E D R

WK145		Canberra B.2	Fire
XN657		Sea Vixen D.3	Stored

V A L L E Y

XE874	8582M	Vampire T.11	Gate
XL392	8745M	Vulcan B.2A	Fire
XP361	8731M	Whirlwind HAR.10	Gate
XR534	8578M	Gnat T.1	Gate
XT772	8805M	Wessex HU.5	BDRT

Part 4

CHANNEL ISLES

GUERNSEY

Airport

G-ASHV		Aztec 250B	Air Scouts
G-BAZJ		Herald 209	Fire
G-BCYC		Trislander	Fuselage
TX192		Anson C.19	Poor state
WJ350		Sea Prince C.2	Fire
WL131	7751M	Meteor F.8	Nose

Elsewhere

G-AOAC	Tiger Moth	Restn
G-ASTH	Mooney M.20	Stored
G-ATEP	EAA Biplane	Stored
G-ATHN	Noralpha	Stored

JERSEY

Airport

G-AOJD	Viscount 802	Fire
G-ASDO	Baron A55	2498 Sqn ATC
G-BBXJ	Herald 203	Fire

Elsewhere

G-APWG	Herald 201	Nose

Part 5

NORTHERN IRELAND

B E L F A S T
(County Antrim) <u>CCF</u>, Campbell College

XD525	7882M Vampire T.11	Pod

B E L F A S T   A I R P O R T
(Or Aldergrove, County Antrim)

G-AVFE	Trident 2E	Fire
WS840	7969M Meteor NF.14	Restn
WT486	8102M Canberra T.4	Fire
XR700	8589M Jet Provost T.4	Nose
XT456	Wessex HU.5	BDRT
XT669	8894M Wessex HC.2	Inst

**B E L F A S T   H A R B O U R
A I R P O R T**
(Or Sydenham, County Down)

G-BSBH	Short SD.330	Stored
1317	T-27 Tucano	Test bed

B I S H O P ' S   C O U R T
(County Down)

VP957	8822M Devon C.2/2	Inst

H O L Y W O O D
<u>Ulster Folk and Transport Museum</u>
The Museum is open October to April, Monday to Saturday 1100 to 1700, Sunday 1400 to 1700 and May to September, Monday to Saturday 1100 to 1800, Sunday 1400 to 1800. Contact : Ulster Folk and Transport Museum, Cultra Manor, Holywood, Northern Ireland BT18 0EU. Tel 02317 5411

G-AJOC	Messenger 2A	Stored
G-AKEL	Gemini 1A	Restn
G-AKGE	Gemini 3C	Restn

G-AKLW	Sealand	Stored
G-AOUR	Tiger Moth	Stored
G-ARTZ	McCandless M-2	Stored
G-ATXX	McCandless M-4	-
BGA.470	Nimbus I	Stored
IAHC 6	Ferguson Monoplane rep	-
IAHC 9	Ferguson Monoplane	
	Replica, stored	
VH-UUP G-ACUX	Scion I	Stored
XG905	Short SC.1	-

M O V E N I S
(Near Garvagh, County Londonderry)

G-AWJA	Cessna 182L	Fuselage

M U L L A G H M O R E
(County Londonderry)

G-AYTB	Rallye Club	Wreck
G-BFPC	AA-5B Tiger	Wreck

N E W T O W N A R D S
(County Down) <u>Ulster Aviation Society</u>
Enquiries to : Raymond Burrows, 20 Carrowreagh Gardens, Dundonald, Belfast BT16 0TW.

JV482	Wildcat V	Restn
WN108	Sea Hawk FB.3	-
WZ549	8118M Vampire T.11	
XG736	Sea Venom FAW.22	Restn

<u>Airfield</u>

G-BBTT	Cessna F.150L	Fuselage

U P P E R   B A L L I N D E R R Y
(Near Crumlin, County Antrim)

G-AERV	Whitney Straight	Restn

Part 6

EIRE

ABBEYSHRULE
(West of Mullingar, off the L18, Westmeagh)

EI-ABU	Spartan II	Stored
EI-ANN	Tiger Moth	Stored
EI-AOP	Tiger Moth	Restn
EI-ATL	Champion 7AC	Spares
EI-AUP	Rallye Club	Wreck
EI-AVB	Champion 7AC	Restn
EI-BAG	Cessna 172A	Stored
EI-BDB	Rallye Club	Fuselage
EI-BDH	Rallye Club	Stored
EI-BGN	Rallye Club	Fuselage
EI-BKE	Super Rallye	Wreck

CARBURY
(Kildare)

IAHC 3	Mignet HM.14	Stored

CASEMENT
(Or Baldonnel, west of Dublin, County Dublin)

164		Chipmunk T.20	Stored
181		Provost T.51	Dump
189A		Provost T.51	Dump
193		Vampire T.55	Pod
198	XE977	Vampire T.11	Gate
221	No 79	CM-170 Magister	Inst
		Alouette III	Inst
	G-ARLU	Cessna 172B	Inst

CASTLEBRIDGE
(North of Wexford, County Wexford)

EI-ALP	Avro Cadet	Stored
VM659	Cadet TX.2	Stored

COONAGH
(West of Limerick, off the N18, Limerick)

F-BGOO G-AKSY	Auster 5	Stored

CORK AIRPORT
(South of the City, County Cork)

EI-AUT	F.1A Aircoupe	Restn
G-ACMA	Leopard Moth	Stored
N4422P	Geronimo	Stored

DUBLIN
Irish Aviation Museum, store

EI-AOH	Viscount 808	Nose
IAHC 1	Mignet HM.14	Loan
G-AOGA	Aries 1	Stored
G-ANPC	Tiger Moth	Frame
34	Magister	Stored
141	Anson XIX	Stored
183	Provost T.51	Stored
191	Vampire T.55	Stored

DUBLIN AIRPORT
(Or Collinstown, north of the city on the N1, County Dublin)

EI-ALU	Cadet	Stored
EI-AMK	J/1 Autocrat	Stored
EI-ARY	Cessna F.150H	Wreck
EI-AUH	Cessna F.172H	Fuselage
EI-AYJ	Cessna 182P	Wreck
EI-BEO	Cessna 310Q II	Stored
EI-BGO	Canadair CL-44J	Fire
EI-BIA	Cessna FA.152	Wreck
G-BHIA	Cessna F.152-II	Stored

GALWAY AIRPORT
(County Galway)

EI-BBR	BN-2A-26 Islander	Wreck

GORMANSTON
(County Dublin)

168	Chipmunk T.20	Restn
172	Chipmunk T.20	Stored
199	Chipmunk T.20	Spares

KILDIMO
(County Limerick) Scrapyard

EI-AOS	Cessna 310B	-
EI-ATH	Cessna F.150J	-
EI-AUD	Rallye Club	-
EI-AUV	Aztec 250C	-
EI-BDM	Aztec 250D	-
EI-BFE	Cessna F.150G	-
EI-BJA	Cessna FRA.150L	-
EI-BML	Aztec 250C	-
G-AZGH	Rallye Club	-
HB-CFI	Cessna F.172P	-
	MS.230 (?)	-

KILMOON
(County Meath)

EI-AKM	J-3C-65 Cub	Stored
EI-BCO	J-3C-65 Cub	Stored

PORTLAOISE
(County Laoise)

IAHC 2	Aldritt Monoplane	Stored

POWERSCOURT
(South of Dublin, County Wicklow)

EI-AMY	J/1N Alpha	Spares

RATHCOOLE
(County Cork)

EI-AFF	BA Swallow II	Stored
EI-AFN	BA Swallow II	Stored
EI-ASU	Terrier 2	Stored

SHANNON AIRPORT

EI-AYW	Aztec 250C	Stored
G-AWUP	Cessna F.150H	Stored
N3760D	Caribou	Stored
4R-ALB	Boeing 707-321B	Fire

Industrial Training School

EI-BHU	Skipper	Wreck
HB-CCW	Cessna F.172N	Wreck
SP-AFX	Wilga 35	Wreck

SLIGO
(County Sligo)

IAHC 7	Sligo Concept	Stored
IAHC 8	O'Hara Autogyro	Stored

WATERFORD AIRPORT
(South east of the town, County Waterford)   South East Aviation Enthusiasts

G-AOIE		Douglas DC-7C	—
VP-BDF		Boeing 707-321	Nose
		Gemini	Cockpit
173		Chipmunk T.20	—
176"	VP-YKF	Dove 6	—
184		Provost T.51	—
187		Vampire T.55	—
192		Vampire T.55	Pod

Part 7

RAF OVERSEAS

West Germany

B R U G G E N

XE608	8717M	Hunter F.6A	BDRT
XL566	8891M	Hunter T.7	BDRT
XM970	8529M	Lightning T.4	Decoy
XM973	8528M	Lightning T.4	Decoy
XN783	8526M	Lightning F.2A	Decoy
XN789	8527M	Lightning F.2A	Decoy
XN792	8525M	Lightning F.2A	BDRT
XP403	8690M	Whirlwind HAR.10	BDRT
XS901		Lightning F.6	BDRT
XV358	8658M	Buccaneer S.2C	BDRT
XX822"	8563M	Jaguar GR.1	Gate

D E T M O L D

XL739	Skeeter AOP.12	Gate
XS571	Wasp HAS.1	BDRT
XV627	Wasp HAS.1	BDRT
XW615	Scout AH.1	BDRT

G A T O W
(West Berlin)

TG503	8555M	Hastings T.5	Gate
WF382	8872M	Varsity T.1	Gate
WJ491		Valetta C.1	Fire
A65-69	ZD215	Dakota III	Gate

G U T E R S L O H

XF949"	XG152	Hunter F.6A	BDRT
XM244	8202M	Canberra B(I).8	Fire
XP358		Whirlwind HAR.10	BDRT
XR504"	XT467	Wessex HU.5	BDRT
XV278		Harrier GR.1	WLT
XZ989	8849M	Harrier GR.3	BDRT
		Harrier GR.3	BDRT

H I L D E S H E I M

XP852		Scout AH.1	BDRT
XT438	A2704	Wasp HAS.1	BDRT

L A A R B R U C H

XJ673"	XE606	Hunter F.6A	Gate
XM264	8227M	Canberra B(I).8	Gate
XN732	8519M	Lightning F.2A	Decoy, 'MiG-21' guise
XN788	8543M	Lightning F.2A	BDRT
XN956	8059M	Buccaneer S.1	BDRT
XR758		Lightning F.6	BDRT

M I N D E N

XP898	Scout AH.1	BDRT
XX376	Gazelle AH.1	BDRT

S O E S T

XP897	Scout AH.1	BDRT
XT436	Wasp HAS.1	BDRT

W I L D E N R A T H

WV701	8936M	Pembroke C.1	Inst
XF418	8842M	Hunter F.6A	BDRT
XM995	8542M	Lightning T.4	Decoy
XN778	8537M	Lightning F.2A	Decoy
XR727	8962M	Lightning F.6	BDRT

Cyprus

A K R O T I R I

WJ768		Canberra B.6(mod)	Fire
XJ437	8788M	Whirlwind HAR.10	BDRT
XS929		Lightning F.6	Gate

L A R N A C A

XD184	8787M	Whirlwind HAR.10	Gate

Falkland Islands

M O U N T P L E A S A N T
A I R P O R T

A-529	FMA Pucara	Stored
AE-410	Bell UH-1H	Stored

S A L V A D O R S E T T L E M E N T

XM666	Whirlwind HAR.9	Hulk

Gibraltar

N O R T H F R O N T

XM571	8812M	Vulcan K.2	Gate
		Hunter	BDRT

Hong Kong

S E K K O N G

XP887	Scout AH.1	Dump
XP906	Scout AH.1	Fire
XR500	Wessex HC.2	Dump
XT618	Scout AH.1	Dump
	Scout AH.1	Dump
	Scout AH.1	Dump
	Scout AH.1	Dump

OFF DUTY

During 1988 the RAF's Historic Aircraft Committee took on the thorny question of 'gate guardian' Spitfires and decided to take all of them so employed 'off duty'. As the Pocket Edition of **Wrecks & Relics** goes to press, the Spitfires were being removed from their posts and 'plastic' full-size Hurricane or Spitfire replicas were being erected at the gates of bases chosen to receive them.

The bulk of the Spitfires were to go to St Athan for inspection and subsequent disposal/relocation arrangements. To spread the work, Shawbury is also reported to involved in this work. Because it would not be right to list these aircraft at their previous bases, it has been decided for purposes of continuity to list the Spitfires involved here as it is clear that the remainder of 1989 and early 1990 will see much activity on this front. (The 12th Edition of **Wrecks & Relics** will list all movements in detail.)

To 'finance' the 'plastic' replacements the RAF has entered an agreement with Historic Flying Ltd (HFL) of Cambridge, who have taken five real airframes in return. (HFL are also financing a P-40 Kittyhawk and a Beaufort for the RAF Museum.) HFL's Spitfires will be worked on in a workshop in East Anglia, but for now are listed below.

Serial	'M' No	Type	'Guarded'	Replacement	Disposal
BM597	5718M	Spitfire Vb	Church Fenton	Replica	HFL, Cambridge
EP120	8070M	Spitfire Vb	Wattisham	None	
LA198	7118M	Spitfire F.21	Leuchars	None	
LA255	6490M	Spitfire F.21	Wittering	Replica	
PK624	8072M	Spitfire F.24	Abingdon	None	
PK664	7759M	Spitfire F.22	Binbrook	None, base closed	St Athan
PM651	7758M	Spitfire PR.XIX	Benson	Replica	
RW382	8075M	Spitfire XVI	Uxbridge	Replica	HFL, Cambridge
RW393	7293M	Spitfire XVI	Edinburgh	Replica	
SL542	8390M	Spitfire XVI	Coltishall	Replica (Hurricane)	
SL674	8392M	Spitfire XVI	Biggin Hill	Replicas (one of each)	
TB252	8073M	Spitfire XVI	Bentley Priory	Replica	HFL, Cambridge
TD248	7246M	Spitfire XVI	Sealand	Hunter	via HFL to Earls Colne
TE476	8071M	Spitfire XVI	Northolt	Replica	HFL, Cambridge

(Life-long followers of **Wrecks & Relics** may like the parallel that in the very first edition, published in May 1961, all Spitfires were not included as they had recently been listed in 'Flypast', the journal of the original publishers, the Merseyside Society of Aviation Enthusiasts. Nearly thirty years later a 'grandchild' of that first edition is engaged in a similar operation!)

USEFUL ADDRESSES

As an abridged version, it would be impossible to give here the vast array of addresses that the 'big' volume does. Herewith a listing of bodies and organisations that the compiler considers most useful to the reader. Included here are the enthusiast organisations that publish magazines that most cater for the **Wrecks & Relics** follower.

Air-Britain
[Publishers of the monthly 'Air-Britain News']
Membership Secretary, Howard Nash, 11 Thurlestone, Thundersley, Benfleet, Essex, SS7 3YW

British Aircraft Preservation Council
Secretary, David Reader, 151 Marshalswick Lane, St Albans, Herts, AL1 4UX

British Aviation Archaeology Council
Chairman, David Stansfield, School House, Sharneyford, Bacup, Lancs, OL13 9UQ

British Aviation Research Group
[Publishers of the monthly 'British Aviation Review']
Membership Secretary, Paul Hewins, 8 Nightingale Road, Woodley, Berks, RG5 3LP

Humberside Aviation Society
[Publishers of the monthly 'Humberside Air Review']
Secretary, Paul Wild, 4 Bleach Yard, Beverley, North Humberside, HU17 7HG

Irish Aviation Historical Council
Information Officer, Joe McDermott, 151 Cloncliffe Avenue, Dublin 3, Eire

Midland Counties Publications
[Publishers of the 'Wrecks & Relics' series]
24 The Hollow, Earl Shilton, Leicester, Leics, LE9 7NA. (And see end papers)

Warbirds Worldwide
[Publishers of the quarterly of the same name]
Paul Coggan, PO Box 4, Shirebrook, Mansfield, Notts, NG20 8PB

LOCATIONS INDEX

Alternative names for locations are given in brackets. Countries and Counties are given in bold. Entries in the 'RAF Overseas' section are <u>not</u> given here.

"We apologise for the inconvenience"

British Military Aircraft Serials
1878-1987

This book is a completely revised, updated and redesigned edition of what has become a standard reference work. It is a complete guide to the aircraft acquired by the British Services since 1878. It includes serial numbers, quantities ordered, precise aircraft type and mark or model, remarks on conversions, modifications and builders. Lists all airships, aerplanes, seaplanes, flying boats, amphibians, autogyros, helicopters, gliders and hovercraft acquired by purchase, impressment, presentation or capture. Cancelled orders are also included. This edition contains over 200 photographs and appendices that include Maintenance Serials and the Air-Min series used for aircraft captured during the Second World War.

The author is, Bruce Robertson, who has many highly respected works on various aspects of aviation published.

Price £10.95   Now available.

European Wrecks & Relics

For twenty-five years, the ever-popular *Wrecks & Relics* has reviewed preserved, instructional and derelict aircraft in the UK and Eire and has become an eagerly-awaited 'bible' for enthusiasts.

Now, at last, there is to be a companion covering Europe, from Iceland right across to Cyprus (but excluding Eastern Europe at least for this first edition); nineteen countries are included – not only the current scene in each, but augmented by historical notes recording what has been happening over the past few years and some aircraft alas lost forever. The diversity of types and ranges of locations are a constant source of surprise, so not only will this be a thoroughly well-thumbed reference, it's a fascinating read in its own right. There is a good deal of really fresh information in here and new material is flooding in as we go to press with this 'Pocket Edition' of the UK *Wrecks & Relics*.

Approximately 200 black and white photos covering a wide range of locations and aircraft types. Full colour laminated hardback cover. A5 size, probably 320 pages (64 are photo pages).

Price provisionally £12.95   (ISBN 0 904597 76 8)   Publication July/August 1989.

Aviation & Military Books by Post

We stock many thousands of books from all over the world for world-wide mail order. Our quick turn-round and superb packing is unrivalled. Free informative and illustrated catalogue on request - write or 'phone –

Midland Counties Publications
24 The Hollow
Earl Shilton
Leicester
LE9 7NA
Telephone: 0455 - 47091/47256

High Ground Wrecks

This is a brand new, totally revised updated and re-designed third edition of what has become acknowledged as the 'bible' of aircraft crash sites in the more remote parts of the United Kingdom and Ireland. It is not only an ideal guide for hill-walkers and wreck hunters, but an intrinsically fascinating documentation of both wartime and peacetime aircraft operations and the hazards facing the crews. Each of fifteen major areas has a descriptive narrative, followed by a listing of sites with aircraft type, serial, unit, location, crash date and details. There are over 60 photographs.

The author is David Smith, a regular contributor to the pages of *Flypast*, *Aviation News* and *After the Battle* magazines, and author of two of the *Action Stations* series of books on UK airfields.

Price £4.95   Now available

Wrecks & Relics 10th Edition

Each edition of *Wrecks & Relics* relies heavily on the edition before it in order to paint an accurate picture of the two-year span of events at every location the UK and Eire. If you have not got the 10th edition (which celebrated 25 years of publication of the title), you will be pleased to know that limited stocks of the work are still available from Midland Counties Publications, priced £8.50 (including post and packing).

WARBIRDS
W O R L D W I D E

The top quality journal on the restoration and operation of ex-military aircraft published quarterly at the end of February, May, August and November. Printed on glossy paper with laminated colour covers, each issue includes approx 120 b/w photos and six pages of colour photos. 48pp A4.

Issue 1: Project Vulcan; Corsair NX1337A; Australia's last Spitfire; Blenheim experience; Albatross HU-16 restoration; Bearcat survivors; MiG-15; Tico '87 warbirds meet. . .£3.95

Issue 2: B-17 G-FORT goes home; Benson's Me109; Hispano Ha.1112MIL; Me109 survivors; 'Empire of the Sun' film; SAAF T-6s; Blenheim swansong; Baghdad Furies. . . .£3.95

Issue 3: The Fighter Collection; P-47 pilot report; VAT's Vampire/Venom; SAAF Harvard Flight; Reno Unlimited Race results; J Sandberg's 'Tsunami' racer £3.95

Issue 4: Texas Air Museum; Fw190F-8 rebuild; Mosquito to Miami; P-51 review; Mitchell round-up; Harvard formation team; Liquid-cooled Hawks part 2; US Gnats £3.95

Issue 5: Old Flying Machine Company; making the 'Battle of Britain' film; Military Austers; Ventura Adventure pt.2; Bombertown, Florida; Wirraway rebuilders report . . .£3.95

Issue 6: Warbirds at Oshkosh 1988; Bombertown part 2; Yak F-AZNN restoration; making of 'Battle of Britain' film part 2; 50th anniversary of the T-6; Douglas Skyraider£3.95

Issue 7: Lone Star Hellcat; Tigercat round-up; Reno Unlimited report 1988; 'Battle of Britain' film aircraft list; Sea Fury Racing at Reno; Spitfires in from the cold £3.95

Issue 8: Flying the Corsair; Charles Church Spitfires; Tempests part 1; Warbirds of Great Britain; Mustang Summer; Worldwide aircraft recovery; Venom rebuild; Jets . . .£3.95

Issue 9: Plane Sailing's Catalina and Tigercat; Stearman across the USA; P-38 Lightning survivors; Chino report; Old Flying Machine Company Corsair pilot report. £4.50

Mustangs Worldwide. A 'special' surveys the remaining P-51s around the world, plus features of Dominican P-51s; the rise and fall of 'Silver Dollar'; Mustang cockpits etc . .£3.95

Jets. A second 'special' devoted to the first generation jets: Flying the Lightning; 'Hunter One' collection; F-86 Sabre review; RAAF's F-86; Fouga Magister; MiG-21 . . . . .£3.95

Wrecks & Relics 11th Edition

This '1989 Pocket Edition' of *Wrecks & Relics* is intended as an updated and handy version of the main volume, which is published biennially.

The 11th Edition is still available and its 224 pages contain a much more detailed survey of all the reserved instructional and derelict airframes in the UK and Eire, as well as on RAF bases overseas, the BAPC/SAPC registers, type and location indexes. There is also a fascinating collection of seventy varied photographs included in this durable laminated hardback.

Still available at £7.95 – post free from Midland Counties Publications.

Wrecks & Relics 12th Edition

The next full-blown edition of *Wrecks & Relics* is planned for publication in Spring 1990 – watch our magazine adverts and catalogues for details nearer the time.
In the Meantime, a reminder for contributors – whose efforts are much appreciated and are the life-blood of the book – that the CLOSING DATE for information and photos is 31 DECEMBER 1989.